On The Construction, Organization, And General Arrangements Of Hospitals For The Insane

STATE HOSPITAL FOR THE INSANE FOR 250 PATIENTS.

ON THE

CONSTRUCTION, ORGANIZATION

AND

GENERAL ARRANGEMENTS

OF

HOSPITALS FOR THE INSANE.

———

BY

THOMAS S. KIRKBRIDE, M.D.,

PHYSICIAN TO THE PENNSYLVANIA HOSPITAL FOR THE INSANE.

———

PHILADELPHIA.
1854.

C O N T E N·T S.

ON CONSTRUCTION.

	PAGE
Preliminary Remarks	1
Public Hospitals	4
Private Institutions	5
County Hospitals	5
Association of Medical Superintendents of American Institutions for the Insane	5
Appointment of Building Commissioners	6
Site for a Hospital for the Insane	6
Amount of Land	7
Supply of Water	8
Drainage	8
Enclosures	9
Patients' Yards	10
Size of the Building	10
Position, Form and General Arrangements	11
Number of Patients in a Ward	14
Cellar	14
Materials of Walls	14
Plastering	15
Security from Fire	15
Roof	15
Size of Rooms	15
Height of Ceilings	15
Floors	16
Doors	16
Locks	16
Windows and Window Guards	17
Inside Window Screens	18
Stairs	18
Associated Dormitories	18
Infirmaries	19
Bath Rooms	19
Water Closets	20
Sinks	21
Urinals	21
Ward Drying Rooms	21
Water Pipes	22
Dust Flues	22
Soiled Clothes Hoppers	22
Kitchens and Distribution of Food	22
Dumb Waiters	23
Speaking Tubes	23
Heating and Ventilation	23
Lighting	28
Washing Arrangements	29
Drying do	29
Ironing do	29
Baking do	29
Farm Buildings	29

PAGE

Cost of a State Hospital............................... 30
Description of Plates................................ 31
Height of Ceilings in Plan 34
Width of Corridors in do............................ 34
Size of Rooms in   do............................ 34
Remarks on the Plan................................. 34

ON ORGANIZATION AND GENERAL ARRANGEMENTS.

Preliminary Remarks................................. 37
List of Officers..................................... 38
Trustees... 38
Treasurer.. 40
Physician.. 40
Assistant Physicians................................ 44
Steward... 44
Matron 45
Chaplain 46
Consulting Physicians 46
Supervisors 47
Teachers.. 47
Attendants... 48
Night Watch 49
Seamstresses....................................... 51
Farmers... 51
Gardeners 51
Engineer and Firemen 51
Carriage Driver 51
Carpenter 51
Jobber 51
Baker... 51
Domestics 51
Remarks on the number employed and their Compensation 51
Schedule of a complete Organization with rate of Com-
    pensation..................................... 52
Residence of the Physician 54
Hospital Furniture................................. 56
Classification of Patients 58
Should Curables and Incurables be separated? 58
Separation of the Sexes............................. 59
Restraint and Seclusion............................. 60
Labor, Out-Door Exercise and Amusements............ 61
Means of Extinguishing Fire 63
Supervision of Hospitals for the Insane 64
Provision for Insane Criminals...................... 65
Visitors 67
Admission of Patients 70
Importance of a correct Nomenclature............... 72

APPENDIX.

Propositions relative to the Construction of Hospitals for
    the Insane.................................... 76
Propositions relative to the Organization of Hospitals for
    the Insane 78

CONSTRUCTION AND ORGANIZATION

OF

HOSPITALS FOR THE INSANE.

The proper custody and treatment of the insane, are now recognized as among the duties which every State owes to its citizens; and as a consequence, structures for the special accommodation of those laboring under mental disease, provided at the general expense, and under the supervision of the public authorities, will probably before any long period, be found in every one of the United States.

There is abundant reason why every State should make ample provision, not only for the proper custody, but also for the most enlightened treatment of all the insane within its borders. Most other diseases may be managed at home. Even with the most indigent, when laboring under ordinary sickness, the aid of the benevolent may supply all their wants, and furnish every thing requisite for their comfort and recovery, at their own humble abodes. It is not so, however, with insanity; for the universal experience is that a large majority of all such cases can be treated most successfully among strangers, and very generally, only in institutions specially provided for the management of this class of diseases. It is among the most painful features of insanity, that in its treatment, so many are compelled to leave their families; that every comfort and luxury that wealth or the tenderest affection can give, are so frequently of little avail at home; and that as regards a restoration or the means to be employed, those surrounded with every earthly blessing are placed so nearly on a level with the humblest of their fellow beings.

Although, with great inconvenience, the affluent might provide suitable private accommodations, a large proportion of our best citizens, all

1

in moderate circumstances, no less than those dependent on their daily exertions for support, without some public provision, must be deprived of much that is desirable, almost as completely as the pauper portion of the community. The simple claims of a common humanity, then, should induce each State to make a liberal provision for all its insane, and it will be found that it is no less its interest to do so, as a mere matter of economy, especially as regards the poor.

Of the recent cases of insanity, properly treated, between 80 and 90 per cent recover. Of those neglected or improperly managed, very few get well. Where fifty or one hundred dollars may be required to cure a case, ten times that amount may not be sufficient to support one that is uncured through life. Those who recover may become valuable citizens; if they do not add directly to the wealth of the State, they at least support their families; those who become incurable, are often during a long life, a source of constant expense to the public, and not unfrequently their families also become a public burthen. More than all this, when ample provision is made for all the insane, recent cases are likely to be placed promptly under treatment, and retained in a place of security till they are well. The effect of this, is greatly to increase the ratio of recoveries, and to spare the community a recital of the most atrocious acts committed on the innocent and unoffending, by irresponsible individuals, simply because their friends, or the proper authorities, have neglected the obvious duty of placing them in a place of security, not only to promote their restoration, but for the protection of the public.

The location of a hospital for the insane, its general arrangements and official organization, must ever exert so important an influence on the comfort and happiness of all its patients, on the prospects for a recovery in those that are curable, and of the mental and physical well-being of those that are incurable, that no apology is required for any one, who having some practical knowledge of the subject, desires a general dissemination of the views and conclusions which have resulted from actual experience among those for whom these institutions are specially intended.

The physicians to the hospitals for the insane in the United States, almost invariably exercise a general superintendence of all their departments, and they are so frequently consulted in reference to the details of these institutions, that their opinions can hardly fail to exert an important influence on the character of the buildings hereafter to be erected. In common with his brethren throughout the country, the writer has been frequently honored with these inquiries, and detailed statements of his views on nearly every subject connected with the treatment of the insane have been so often solicited, that he is induced to present some of the results of his experience in the present form, as a convenient mode of answering these questions, and of aiding those who are commencing their investigations on the subject, rather than from any belief that his opinions possess great novelty or particular interest for those who, like himself, are engaged in the care of the insane.

Sixteen years residence among the insane, in three different institutions—the last thirteen of the time being in immediate superintendence of that with which he is now connected,—and the care of more than 2,700 patients under very varied circumstances, joined to a familiarity with the defects as well as the advantages of a majority of the American hospitals, have not failed to settle the writer's own views on most of the subjects that will be referred to. Others, not less interesting, but about which there has seemed to be more uncertainty, have been purposely avoided.

It is pretty generally conceded, that a more convenient style of architecture, and better arrangements, are desirable in most establishments for the care of the insane; and those who have been personally familiar with the losses sustained by imperfect accommodations, and the advantages derived from improved ones, will be sure to be found most anxious to secure a high character to every one of these institutions, without regard to the class of patients they are intended to receive.

No better proof need be given of the necessity for improvements in the construction and arrangements of hospitals for the insane, than the simple fact that some of the very last which have been put up, exhibit in many parts most glaring defects, and that nearly all erected till within a very few years, have required extensive and costly alterations or additions; or if these changes have not been made, the buildings still remain unsuited for the proper and convenient treatment of the patients. Many of these lamentable defects,—which often can scarcely be remedied without actually re-building the hospital,—and the large expenditures of money, in making alterations and improvements, have often resulted almost entirely from the buildings having been planned by persons who, whatever may have been their taste, architectural skill or good intentions, had no knowledge of what is required for the proper care and treatment of the insane.

No reasonable person at the present day, when planning a hospital for the insane, would think it necessary or desirable to propose a building entirely original in its design; for such a structure could hardly fail to loose in usefulness what it gained in novelty. Instead of something entirely new, the object should rather be to profit by the experience of the past, by the knowledge of those who have a practical familiarity with the wants and requirements of the insane, and after a careful study of existing institutions, to combine, as far as possible, all their good features, and especially to avoid their defects and inconveniences.

These institutions, especially when put up under State authority, while having a plain, but still good and agreeable style of architecture, should not involve too large an expenditure of money in their erection; but, nevertheless, should be so conveniently arranged as to be economical in their subsequent management, and should have every possible advantage for the best kind of classification and supervision of their patients, and for their comfort and treatment.

Every one concerned in providing accommodations for the insane, may rely upon the fact being established by all experience, that the best kind of hospitals,—not only best built, but with the most perfect arrangements and fixtures of every kind, and managed in the most liberal and enlightened manner,—are sure to be most economical in the end—(for true economy consists, not only in avoiding all waste and extravagance, but also in doing thoroughly whatever is undertaken)—will fulfil most completely the objects for which they are erected, and ultimately give most satisfaction to every enlightened community.

The plan proposed in the following pages, is for a State hospital to accommodate 250 patients; this number being now almost universally conceded to be as many as should be collected in any one institution. State hospitals, it is to be remembered, are not for the pauper portion of the community alone, but for every class of citizens. All who pay taxes aid in their erection, and all have the right to participate in their advantages, while in most of the States they furnish the only accommodations for the care of any portion of the insane. Except in the vicinity of a few of our largest cities, it is not probable, at least for many years, that any other class of institutions will be put up in any section of the United States; and on that account, it is particulary desirable that public opinion should be settled as to what is indispensable for this description of hospitals. The same plan and arrangements are applicable, however, to the hospitals intended for the insane poor of large cities, and also, with some slight variations, would answer for the corporate institutions, connected with the hospitals for the sick in Philadelphia, New York and Boston.

In nearly all of these different institutions, it is necessary that a strict regard should be had to first cost, and, as before observed, to economy in subsequent management. On these accounts, I propose recommending only what I deem absolutely necessary for the proper accommodation and treatment of the insane in any of the classes of hospitals previously referred to.

There are several variations that might be suggested, where it was proposed to provide the most perfect arrangements, without regard to cost, or to furnish accommodations for the most wealthy in the community; for I know of no reason why an individual who has the misfortune to become insane, should, on that account, be deprived of any comfort or even luxury, that is not improper or injurious, to which he has been accustomed, or which his income will justify. An insane member of a family, wherever he may be, has really a claim for every thing that will contribute to his comfort and gratification, far beyond those who are in health and have so many other resources; and the justice or morality of a different course, as occasionally observed, can not for a single moment bear examination.

The only other class of institutions for the care of the insane, not already referred to, are private establishments belonging to individuals, and having no supervision by boards of managers, or the public authorities. So far as I know, only two or three of this kind have proved successful in the United States; and for various and sound reasons, it is not desirable nor probable, that the number will hereafter be materially increased.

In some sections of the country it has become a matter of interest to the community, and the question has been freely discussed, whether certain classes of the insane may not be as well kept, and more economically, in county hospitals than in State institutions, and whether it is not desirable that such establishments should be provided in connection with the alms houses in many districts of country. The best interests of the indigent insane are closely connected with the proper settlement of this question; and on that account, without entering fully into its discussion, it may not be amiss to remark, that my observations and reflections have entirely satisfied me that nothing could be more improper or injurious than such an attempt to separate the supposed curable and incurable insane. I am also well convinced that no where can the pauper insane, curable or incurable, be properly treated at a less cost than in a well conducted State institution, and that the only case where county hospitals for the insane are desirable, or should be provided, is in the vicinity of large towns, or in very populous counties, which can furnish about one hundred patients, or enough to make it expedient to have a regular organization, with a resident medical superintendent, and all the other arrangements hereafter to be referred to, as proper in a State hospital.

The general principles which should regulate the construction, organization and varied arrangements of hospitals for the insane, are much better understood than formerly, and the unanimous resolutions of "THE ASSOCIATION OF MEDICAL SUPERINTENDENTS OF AMERICAN INSTITUTIONS FOR THE INSANE," show a gratifying degree of unanimity among those engaged in the care of this afflicted class throughout the country.

This association, formed in 1844, and holding annual sessions in different parts of the country, has visited and carefully inspected a large number of institutions, and has among its members the chief medical officers of nearly every respectable institution for the insane on the continent. A series of twenty-six propositions in reference to the construction of hospitals for the insane, adopted by the association at its meeting in Philadelphia, in 1851, have already been recognized as authority by the general and several of the State governments, and by various corporate bodies interested in the welfare of those laboring under mental disease. The plan proposed in the present essay, is intended to be in every respect, fully in accordance with the expressed views of the association, as shown in the propositions just referred to in reference to construction, and also with those subsequently adopted at the meeting at Baltimore, in 1853, in reference to organization, both of which series will be found in the appendix.

Of these propositions, it may be safely asserted, that if carried out in their true spirit, they can not fail to give us institutions of a high order, every way superior to those formerly erected, and it is believed at as small a cost, as can thoroughly effect the objects aimed at by their provision.

Whenever it is seriously proposed to establish a State hospital for the insane, it becomes the friends of this unfortunate class carefully to attend to the first steps taken to promote this object. Those who frame the legislative bills providing for these institutions, frequently have it in their power to do much towards deciding their future character and usefulness, by a careful attention to the nature of the acts which are passed, and by insisting upon a judicious selection of the men who are to choose the site, decide upon the plan, superintend the erection of the building, and control its subsequent management. As great power is commonly placed in the hands of these individuals, it will readily be understood how important it is that they should be men of high character, strict integrity, active benevolence, and of business habits. They should be willing fully to inform themselves of the character and responsibility of the high trust confided to them, and should avoid hastily taking any step which might mar to a greater or less extent, the usefulness of the institution as long as it may exist.

SITE.—When it has been determined to erect a hospital for the insane, the first object to be attended to, by those to whom this important duty has been delegated, is to select a suitable site for the buildings. The utmost caution should be observed in taking this step, on which may depend to no small extent, the future character and usefulness of the institution; for the best style of building and the most liberal organization can never fully compensate for the loss sustained by a location that deprives the patients of may valuable privileges, or subjects them to varied annoyances. It is now well established that this class of hospitals should always be located in the country, not within less than two miles of a town of considerable size, and they should be easily accessible at all seasons. They should, if possible, be near turnpikes or other good roads, or on the line of a railroad. While two or three miles from a town might be named as a good distance on the former, the facilities afforded by a railroad might make ten or twelve miles unobjectionable; for it is the time spent in passing and ease of access, rather than distance, that is most important. Proximity to a town of considerable size has many advantages, as in procuring supplies, obtaining domestic help or mechanical workmen, and on account of the various matters of interest not elsewhere accessible to the patients. In selecting a site, facility of access from the districts of country from which the patients will be principally derived, should never be overlooked.

The building should be in a healthful, pleasant and fertile district of country; the land chosen should be of good quality and easily tilled; the surrounding scenery should be of a varied and attractive kind, and the neighborhood should possess numerous objects of an agreeable and interesting character. While the hospital itself should be retired and its privacy fully secured, it is desirable that the views from it should exhibit life in its active forms, and on this account stirring objects at a little distance are desirable. Reference should also be made to the amount of wood and tillable land that may be obtained, to the supply of water, and to the facilities for drainage, and for enclosing the pleasure grounds.

AMOUNT OF LAND.—Every hospital for the insane should possess at least one hundred acres of land, to enable it to have the proper amount for farming and gardening purposes, to give the desired degree of privacy and to secure adequate and appropriate means of exercise, labor and occupation to the patients, for all these are now recognized as among the most valuable means of treatment. Of the total amount, from thirty to fifty acres immediately around the buildings, should be appropriated as pleasure grounds, and should be so arranged and enclosed as to give the patients the full benefit of them, without being annoyed by the presence of visitors or others. It is desirable that several acres of this tract should be in groves or woodland, to furnish shade in Summer, and its general character should be such as will admit of tasteful and agreeable improvements. To enable the patients generally to have the greatest possible amount of benefit from their pleasure grounds, those of the males and females should be entirely distinct; and one of the best means of separating them will be found to be the appropriation of a strip of neutral ground, properly enclosed between them, as a park for various kinds of animals, or to be otherwise handsomely cultivated. While less than one hundred acres should be deemed too little for any institution, many State hospitals having a large number of farmers or working men, will find it useful to possess double that amount; and extensive walks and drives on the hospital premises offer so many advantages, that the possession of a large tract for this purpose alone is often desirable. It is hardly possible under any circumstances, for such an institution to control too much land immediately around it.

SUPPLY OF WATER.—An abundant supply of good water is one of the necessaries of every hospital, and should be secured whatever may be the cost or trouble required to effect it. A very extensive use of baths is among the most important means of treatment, and the large number of water closets that are indespensable in the wards, the great amount of washing that is to be done, as well as various other arrangements requiring a free use of water, and above all, abundant means for extinguishing fire, in case such an accident should occur, make it of the utmost importance that the supply should be permanent and of the most liberal kind.

The daily consumption for all purposes in an institution for 250 patients, will not be much, if any less, than 10,000 gallons, and tanks to contain more than this amount should be placed in the dome or highest part of the building.

When a sufficient elevation can be met with to carry the water to the tanks by gravity, nothing can be better; or a steady water power will be both convenient and economical; but so few sites will be found having either of these advantages, combined with the other requisites for such an institution, and as a steam engine will always be desirable on various other accounts, it will be safe to say that this will be the best reliance in most locations. Horse power is not to be recommended. The water should be distributed to every part of the building, and arrangements should be made to furnish a full supply, both hot and cold, to every ward and in every section of the house. One or two wells near the building, for furnishing drinking water, will be desirable, and a large cistern outside of the hospital should be provided, to secure a supply in case of fire.

DRAINAGE.—All the drainage should be under ground, and in selecting a site, facilities for making this very important arrangement should never be overlooked. All the waste water from the kitchens, sculleries, baths, water closets, &c., should be carried off beneath the surface, and to such a distance as will prevent the possibility of its proving an annoyance to the hospital. All the entrances to the culverts should be trapped, and the culverts should be made so large and with such a descent as will obviate all risks of obstructions. If the rain water from the roof and the surface drainage are taken in another direction, that from the hospital may be made to add greatly to the fertility of the farm; but it is much better to carry all off through the same culvert and loose this advantage, than incur the slightest risk of having the air in the vicinity of the hospital contaminated by these fertilizing arrangements.

ENCLOSURES.—It is desirable that the pleasure grounds and gardens should be securely enclosed, to protect the patients from the gaze and impertinent curiosity of visitors, and from the excitement occasioned by their presence in the grounds.

This enclosure should be of a permanent character, about ten feet high, and so located that it will not be conspicuous, even if it is at all visible from the building. The site, as well as the position of the building on it, should have some reference to this arrangement. If sufficient inequalities of surface exist, the wall or fence, as it may be, should be placed in the low ground, so as not to obstruct the view; but if the country is too level to admit of this, the same end may be attained by placing the wall in the centre of a line of excavation of sufficient depth to prevent its having an unpleasant appearance, and yet be entirely effective. Although the first cost of a wall will be about double that of a fence of the proper kind, still its durability and greater efficiency in every respect, will make it cheaper in the end. The amount of land thus enclosed should never be less than thirty acres, while forty or even fifty acres will be a more desirable amount, so that the pleasure grounds of the male and female patients, which, as before observed, should be entirely distinct, may be sufficiently extensive. Important as I regard the permanent enclosure of extensive pleasure grounds and gardens, in the manner suggested, as protecting the patients from improper observation, keeping out intruders, enlarging the liberty of the insane generally, securing various improvements from injury, and permitting labor to be used as a remedy for more patients than could otherwise be done, still it is proper to add, that high walls around small enclosures, and in full view from the buildings, are even less desirable than a simple neat railing, which would neither keep determined visitors out, nor active patients in. The first of these objects—keeping the public out,—it must not be forgotten, is the prominent one thought of in recommending a wall to be placed around the pleasure grounds of a hospital. The presence and watchfulness of intelligent attendants must still be the grand reliance to prevent the escape of patients, and I regard any arrangement that does away with the necessity of constant vigilance, undesirable about a hospital for the insane.

Patients' Yards.—Although it does not seem to me desirable to have a large number of private yards in immediate connection with a hospital for the insane, it will still be found convenient to have two for each sex, of a large size, well provided with brick walks, shade trees and such other modes of protection from the sun and weather as may be deemed useful. These yards enable many patients, who at certain periods wish to aviod the greater publicity of the grounds, to have the benefit of the open air, and to take exercise at hours when the attendants cannot conveniently leave the wards; but most of the patients should have a more active and longer continued kind of exercise than these yards afford. They should look to the walks in the open fields and about the grounds, which can readily be made a mile long for each sex, for their principal exercise. Four-fifths of all the patients will, under proper regulations, be able to take walks of this kind for at least a couple of hours morning and afternoon, at all seasons; and in warm weather, when proper summer houses and seats are provided, they may thus profitably spend one half the entire day in the open air. It is always much better for patients to be comfortably seated in a pleasant parlor or hall, at any season of the year, than to be lying on the ground, or otherwise soiling their clothes, and exposing themselves to the risk of taking cold, as is very apt to be the case, when certain classes are allowed to consult their own pleasure as to the mode of passing their time while in the small yards, adjoining the building.

Size of the Building.—A suitable site having been selected, it will next become necessary to decide upon the size of the institution. Whatever differences of opinion may have formerly existed on this point, I believe there are none at present. All the best authorities agree that the number of insane confined in one hospital, should not exceed two hundred and fifty, and it is very important that at no time should a larger number be admitted than the building is calculated to accommodate comfortably, as a crowded institution cannot fail to exercise an unfavorable influence on the welfare of its patients. The precise number that may be properly taken care of in a single institution, will vary somewhat, according to the ratio of acute cases received, and of course to the amount of personal attention required from the chief medical officer. In State institutions, when full, at least one half of all the cases will commonly be of a chronic character, and require little medical treatment. Even when thus proportioned, 250 will be found to be as many as the medical superintendent can visit properly every day, in addition to the performance of his other duties. When the proportion of acute or recent cases is likely to be much greater than that just referred to, the number of patients should be proportionately reduced, and two hundred will then be found to be a preferable maximum. While no more patients should be received into any hospital than can be visited daily by the chief medical officer, it is desirable that the number should be sufficiently large to give an agreeable company to each class, and to permit a variety of occupations and amusements that would prove too costly for a small institution, unless filled with patients paying a very high rate of board, or possessed of some permanent endowment. It might be supposed that institutions for a much larger number of patients than has been recommended, could be supported at a less relative cost, but this is not found to be the case. There is always more difficulty in superintending details in a very large hospital,—there are more sources of waste and loss, improvements are apt to be relatively more costly, and without great care on the part of the officers, the patients will be less comfortable.

Whenever an existing State institution built for 250 patients, contains that number, and does not meet the wants of the community, instead of crowding it, and thereby rendering all its inmates uncomfortable, or materially enlarging its capacity by putting up additional buildings, it will be found much better at once to erect an entirely new institution in another section of the State; for under any circumstances, the transfer of acute cases from a great distance, is an evil of serious magnitude and constantly deplored by those who have the care of the insane.

POSITION, FORM AND GENERAL ARRANGEMENTS.—The size of the building having been determined, its form and general arrangements will next require attention; and no plan, however beautiful its exterior may appear, nor how apparently ingenious its interior may seem, should ever be adopted without having been first submitted to the inspection and received the approval of some one or more physicians who have had a large practical acquaintance with the insane, and who are thoroughly familiar with the details of their treatment, as well as with the advantages and defects of existing hospitals for their accommodation. So different from ordinary buildings or other public structures are hospitals for the insane, that it is hardly possible for an architect, however skillful, or a board of commissioners, however intelligent and well disposed, unaided, to furnish such an institution with all the conveniences and arrangements indispensable for the proper care and treatment of its patients. No desire to make a beautiful and picturesque exterior should ever be allowed to interfere with the internal arrangements. The interior should be first planned, and the exterior so managed as not to spoil it in any of its details.

Although it is not desirable to have an elaborate or costly style of architecture, it is, nevertheless, really important that the building should be in good taste, and that it should impress favorably not only the patients, but their friends and others who may visit it. A hospital for the insane should have a cheerful and comfortable appearance, every thing repulsive and prison-like should be carefully avoided, and even the means of effecting the proper degree of security should be masked, as far as possible, by arrangements of a pleasant and attractive character. For the same reason, the grounds about the building should be highly improved and tastefully ornamented; a variety of objects of interest should be collected around it, and trees and shrubs, flowering plants, summer-houses, and other pleasing arrangements, should add to its attractiveness. No one can tell how important all these may prove in the treatment of patients, nor what good effects may result from first impressions thus made upon an invalid on reaching a hospital,—one who perhaps had left home for the first time, and was looking forward to a gloomy, cheerless mansion, surrounded by barren, uncultivated grounds for his future residence, but on his arrival finds every thing neat, tasteful and comfortable. Nor is the influence of these things on the friends of patients unimportant; they cannot fail to see that neither labor nor expense is spared to promote the happiness of the patients, and they are thus led to have a generous confidence in those to whose care their friends have been entrusted, and a readiness to give a steady support to a liberal course of treatment.

Great care should be observed in locating the building, that every possible advantage may be derived from the views and scenery adjacent, and especially from the parlors and other rooms occupied during the day. The prevailing winds of summer may also be made to minister to the comfort of the inmates, and the grounds immediately adjacent to the hospital should have a gradual descent in all directions, to secure a good surface drainage.

For an institution like that under consideration, I believe the best and most economical form will be found to be a centre building with wings on each side, so arranged as to give ample accommodations for the resident officers and their families, and for the classification and comfort of the patients. A building having a basement above ground, and two stories above this, will generally be adopted on account of its being less expensive and of smaller extent than one of only two stories. The centre building and projecting portions of the wings, may be carried up a few feet higher, but the wards should never be. In the highest part of the structure, as in a dome, the water tanks should be provided for.

In the centre building should be the kitchens, main store rooms, a reception room for patients, a general business office, superintendent's office, medical office and library, visiting rooms for friends of patients, a public parlor and managers' room, the lecture room and chapel, and the apartments for the superintending physician's family, and for the other officers of the institution,

The wings should be so arranged as to have eight distinct classes of each sex; each class should occupy a separate ward, and each ward should have in it a parlor, a dining room with a dumb waiter connected with it, and a speaking tube leading to the kitchen or some other central part of the basement story, a corridor, single lodging rooms for patients, an associated dormitory for not less than four beds, communicating with an attendant's chamber, one or two rooms of sufficient size for a patient with a special attendant, a clothes room, a bath room, a wash and sink room, and a water closet. There should also be provided for each sex in their appropriate wings, at least one infirmary for patients who are too ill to remain in their own chambers, two work rooms, a museum and reading room, a school room, a series of drying closets, at least one on each story, and various other fixtures, the general character, position and arrangement of which will be more particularly referred to when describing the accompanying plan, in which they will all be found provided for. The parlors may be dispensed with in the wards for the most excited patients, but not elsewhere, and all the other conveniences suggested will be as necessary for them as any other class.

Although a forced ventilation is deemed indispensable in every hospital for the insane, still a natural ventilation should never be neglected. In most parts of the United States, during one half the year, there is a comfort in the fresh cool breezes that may often be made to pass through the wards, that can not be too highly estimated, and every precaution should be taken to derive full advantage from them. The darkest, most cheerless, and worst ventilated parts of such establishments, will generally be found to be where a wing joins the centre building, or where one wing comes directly in contact with another running at right angles to it. The first of these defects, however, it will hereafter be seen, is easily and effectually remedied by leaving on each side an open space of about eight feet, with movable glazed sash extending from near the floor to the ceiling, and which may either be accessible to the patients or be protected by ornamental open wire work, on a line with the corridor, and giving nearly every advantage of light, air and scenery. Behind such a screen, even in the most excited wards, may be placed with entire security, the most beautiful evergreen and flowering plants, singing birds and various other objects, the contemplation of which can not fail to have a pleasant and soothing effect upon every class of patients. To remedy the other difficulty alluded to, instead of allowing a second wing to come directly in contact with the first, it should be placed on a parallel line, but made to recede just so far as will allow its corridor to be open at both extremities, which should also be furnished with movable glazed sashes, to be accessible to the patients, or protected and ornamented as already suggested, according to the class by which it is to be occupied, and other circumstances. I deem these arrangements of great importance, and as being among the most valuable features of the plan under notice.

NUMBER OF PATIENTS IN A WARD.—As the total number of patients designed to be accommodated is 250, the average in each of the sixteen wards would be a little over fifteen, but the number may be varied somewhat by the character of the cases. Of the quiet, or incurable demented, as many as twenty could be taken care of in one ward, with quite as much facility as less than half that number that are highly excited. Patients that are excitable rarely do well in large wards, and better discipline is almost invariably preserved in those that have a small number of inmates. Where seclusion is to be carefully avoided, it becomes particularly important that means should be provided by which even the most highly excited or violent patient may at proper times be out of his room, without being surrounded by a crowd of persons affected like himself. Every one familiar with institutions for the insane, will recall numerous instances of almost daily occurrence, where a single excitable patient introduced into a comparatively quiet ward, will in an hour have almost entirely changed its character.

The basement or first story of the building, should be raised two steps, or about sixteen inches, above the surface of the ground around it, and a cellar should be excavated under the entire structure. The cost of a cellar is trifling, and it is desirable in many respects, but especially in reference to a proper arrangement of the heating apparatus and of the air reservoirs connected with it.

MATERIALS OF WALLS.—A hospital should be constructed of stone or brick, as may be found most convenient and economical. If of stone, the walls may be pointed or stuccoed. If of good brick, they may be painted to give them an agreeable shade of color. Advantage will be found from using hydraulic cement in laying the foundations, and the floor of the whole cellar, if at all disposed to dampness, should be covered with the same material, while lime and sand will answer in other localities.

On account of the great number of flues that will be required, the inner or corridor walls should be not less than eighteen inches thick and constructed of brick. All the flues for heat and ventilation should be carried up in them, and about the whole space will be required for these purposes. The construction of the outer wall with a space between the two courses of brick, where that material is used, is an admirable arrangement for giving a perfectly dry house, and one little affected by sudden changes of temperature. If stone is adopted as the material for the building, those parts especially exposed to dampness should be battened.

PLASTERING.—The plastering throughout should be what is styled a hard finish, and calculated for being scrubbed, whether kept white or painted of some more agreeable shade of color. When rooms are likely to be much abused by patients, the plastering may be very advantageously done with hydraulic cement and sand, and rubbed down so as to be perfectly smooth. The color can afterwards be made whatever is deemed most desirable.

SECURITY FROM FIRE.—Every precaution should be taken to provide against accidents from fire, and the building should be made as nearly fire proof as circumstances will permit. Brick arching between the different stories would be desirable, but its first cost will probably mostly lead to counter ceiling and other substitutes. The kitchens, in which rooms alone it will be necessary to have fires of any size, should be arched, and the flues leading from them should be constructed with great care. The passages between the different ranges of the wings should be arched, their side walls should run up from the cellar to the roof, they should also have stone floors and iron doors on each side, that could be closed whenever desired. By this arrangement, a fire commencing in any section of the wings, could easily be prevented from spreading to any other, and it might lead to the preservation of all parts of the structure, except the range in which the fire originated.

The buildings should be heated by steam or hot water, and the fires for generating these, should always be in a detached structure, at least one hundred feet from the hospital. This mode of heating and this locality for the large fires, will remove the greatest source of accidents from fire in institutions for the insane.

ROOF.—The roof should be of copper, tin or slate, according to circumstances, and the cornice should project boldly over the walls for their protection, as well as for the sake of a good appearance, and to give a free passage for the water falling on the building. For a flat roof, the best tin thoroughly painted, will probably be found most desirable, although with a good pitch and the slate properly put on, that material will generally give satisfaction.

SIZE OF ROOMS AND HEIGHT OF CEILINGS.—The ceilings in every part regularly occupied by patients, should be at least twelve feet high, and certain parts of the centre building should be more. The corridors of the wings should not be less than twelve feet wide, nor those of the centre building less than fourteen. The parlors and other large rooms should occupy a space equal to about twenty feet square. The single chambers for patients should be made as large as can be well brought about, provided their size is not so great as to lead to two patients being placed in the same room, which ought not to be allowed. Nine feet front by eleven deep will probably be adopted as the best size, although eight by ten is admissible. Great convenience will be found in having in each ward at least one chamber of the size of two single rooms, for the use of a patient with a special attendant.

FLOORS.—The floors of all patient's rooms, without any exception, should be made of well seasoned wood, and counter ceiled to prevent the transmission of sound. When it is expected they will require frequent washing, they may incline very slightly towards the door. Instead of the ordinary washboard, which after a certain time is apt to become a harbor for vermin, cement or mastic painted should be used.

DOORS.—The door of a patient's room should be about 6 feet 8 inches by 2 feet 8 inches, and the frame should be well built in, and thoroughly secured to the wall. Over each door in the principal frame may be an open space, not exceeding five inches in width, which can be closed from the outside when desired, by a moveable board or covered frame.

Although not absolutely necessary in but a small portion of the rooms, it will be found very convenient, to have a neat wicket, secured by a spring lock, in many, if not all of the doors of every ward, to enable the night watch to ascertain the condition of a patient with facility, and without disturbing his rest—to give food or water, or indeed at any time to see what a patient is doing, when it might not be prudent for a single individual to enter the room. What is called a bead and butt door, well made of thoroughly seasoned timber will probably be found one of the best kinds; and if greater security is desired for very violent patients, a casing of boiler iron, firmly secured on the inside and neatly painted will make them entirely safe, and scarcely be observed, or a door, made by having the outside strips perpendicular, and those on the inside horizontal is both cheap and very strong.

The doors may be made to open either into the rooms or corridor as may be deemed most desirable. As the patients' chambers however are small, and as great annoyance and no little danger frequently result from patients' barricading their doors from the inside, so as to render it almost impossible to get access to them, the plan of having the doors to open into the corridor is generally to be preferred. The only advantage resulting from the door opening into the room is that it is less likely to be forced by the efforts of patients from the inside. A good lock and two suitable bolts on the outside however will be found sufficient to prevent risk from this cause, except in very extraordinary cases.

LOCKS.—The locks in a hospital for the insane, are subjected to such constant use, that they should be made with great care, and the parts most likely to wear should be case hardened. This will add but little to the expense and save much trouble afterwards. The keys for the male and female wards should be so entirely different that it will be impossible by any slight alteration to make those for one side open the locks for the other; for it is scarcely necessary to say that male attendants should never be allowed to go into a female ward, which would any where be conclusive proof of a most defective discipline.

The bolts used should be so made, that while having sufficient strength, they should not be conspicuous, and should move without sound.

WINDOWS AND WINDOW GUARDS.—When in order to give a proper architectural effect to the building, the rooms in its centre must have lofty windows, the lower sash may be guarded as hereafter described, while the upper may be left as in an ordinary building. This is sufficient for rooms not regularly used by patients; but if constantly occupied, more attention must be paid to security. Inside shutters, with the upper half permanently closed, and the lower sash properly guarded, sometimes make a very neat arrangement in such rooms.

More care, however, must be observed in reference to patients' chambers and ordinary ward windows. A window about 5 feet 6 inches by 3 feet, will be found of a convenient size, and this will give two sashes, each containing ten lights 5½ by 16 inches. The window seat may be like those in common dwellings, and the window should be placed low enough to make it pleasant to a person sitting in the room. The upper sash should be of cast iron, and well fastened into the frame, while the lower sash, of the same size and pattern, may be of wood, and hung so as to rise and fall throughout its whole extent. The space opposite the lower sash should be protected by a wrought iron window guard, which, if properly made, and painted of a white color, will not prove unsightly. This kind of guard is always to be very strongly secured to the window frame, and in such a manner that the screws may not be accessible to the patients. It should reach to within five inches of the upper sash, and to within the same distance of the frame below. When of a tasteful pattern and neatly made, it will be found very preferable in appearance and quite equal in security, to the unglazed cast iron sash occasionally used, and which after all, when the glass is raised, has to one in the room very much the appearance of two sets of iron bars, placed at right angles, while the wrought iron screen is no more than what is every day seen in certain front windows of some of the best houses in our large cities.

Although there are various other forms of windows in use, which look well and have some advantages, upon the whole I regard that which has been suggested as being the best and most economical for a State institution. If desired, the upper or iron sash may be ballanced, so as to drop five inches, but this adds materially to the expense, and where proper attention is paid to a forced ventilation, can hardly be necessary. By having the glazing done from the inside of the patients' rooms, especially in the upper stories, a great amount of trouble will be saved in the facility with which broken glass, so common an incident in hospitals for the insane, can be repaired.

Where the chamber windows are exposed to a strong sun, Venetian blind shutters on the outside, will be pleasant and useful, or a painted or simple stout muslin verandah awning over each window, will be found to add much to the comfort of the patients, especially in a southern climate.

The verandahs along the whole front, which have been suggested for the South, would prove very costly and could not be used with safety by the patients, unless made so as almost to resemble extensive cages. Good thick walls, with other less costly arrangements, will be found more effectual in promoting the comfort of the patients.

INSIDE WINDOW SCREENS.—For various purposes, it becomes necessary to screen the inside of the windows of a portion of the patients' rooms. It is not only to prevent the breaking of glass when their inmates are excited, and to secure the windows from being opened at improper times, but also as a protection in some very determinedly suicidal cases. For nearly all purposes, a neat wire screen well secured on a hinged frame, and having a spring lock, will be found sufficient, while it admits the air and light, and does not obstruct the view of the scenery beyond. Two or three such guards will be found desirable in every ward, while in those for the most excited, something stronger will be required in a few rooms, such as a close wooden shutter, but with perforations for the admission of light, which I do not think ought to be entirely excluded under any circumstances of excitement. The plan of hinging these window screens is the simplest and cheapest, but in putting up a new building it may easily be arranged to have them slide into the wall, to fall down, or be raised up by weights, as may be preferred. For a very few rooms in the most excited wards, it may be desirable to have only a small window, too narrow to permit the escape of a patient, and too high to be easily accessible.

STAIRS.—All the stairs used by patients should be made of iron, firmly secured to the walls, ample in number, convenient of access, and easy of ascent and descent. They should be so arranged as not to be exposed in any ward. The well around which they are placed, may be made a fine ventilating shaft.

ASSOCIATED DORMITORIES.—A certain portion of the patients may, without disadvantage, be lodged in dormitories containing from four to six beds and communicating by means of a partially glazed door with the room of an attendant. As far as this can be done with safety, it is unquestionably the cheapest mode of providing for patients. About one fourth of all the patients in a State hospital may probably be thus lodged without material disadvantage, and perhaps a twelfth of the whole number may really do better in associated dormitories than in single rooms. These last are principally among the timid, who dread being alone at night, and some of the suicidal, who will remain quietly in bed if another person is in the room, but who could not be trusted without company. The great majority of patients would strenuously object to such an arrangement, just as much in a hospital as they would in a hotel or boarding house; and most of them regard with especial feeling the privilege of enjoying at times the privacy and quiet of their own rooms.

It is convenient to have one or two rooms of the size referred to, in each ward, which if not required or used for this special purpose, will be found particularly convenient in some cases of sickness when it is not desirable to remove a patient from the ward, or when the friends of an individual desire a more spacious apartment than usual, or where a patient has a special attendant lodging in the same room.

INFIRMARIES.—In case of any serious sickness in a hospital for the insane, especially if of a contagious nature, it will be desirable to have at least one room for each sex, of good size, airy, well ventilated, and separated from the wards, where patients can receive more special attention and enjoy greater quiet than in their own chambers. Thus situated, they may be visited by their friends with great facility, without annoyance to the other patients, or any interference with the ordinary operations of the house.

In some cases of protracted illness, especially if likely to terminate fatally, it is a great comfort to the friends of patients, even if not to the patients, to be able to be with them at times, and to render some of those attentions which the character of their disease prevented their receiving at home.

BATH ROOMS.—The bath rooms in each ward should be of about the size of one of the ordinary chambers, and should contain a cast iron bath tub of proper size and shape, with the improved arrangement for admitting hot and cold water through a common opening, just at the lower part of the tub, and for discharging it from a separate one in the bottom.

By drawing a small amount of cold water before the hot is admitted, there is never any vapor in the room. This arrangement also offers great facilities for keeping up any desired temperature, when long continued hot baths are given, without exciting the patient's fears that he is going to be injured, or leading him to suppose that the water is much hotter than it really is, as often happens, when the continued flow of warm water into the tub is directly under the patient's observation. The fixtures for admitting and discharging the water not being over the tub, but entirely beyond it, prevents, in a great measure, the bath tub being used for any but its legitimate purposes. The admission and discharge of the water through different openings, varying very slightly in their level, is preferable to any arrangement which allows one opening to answer both purposes; for in the latter case, the deposits which take place in the pipe are pretty sure to be returned into the tub when the next bath is drawn.

There should also be three marble or enameled cast iron wash basins in one section of the bath room, and furnished with hot and cold water pipes. An arrangement for shower baths and for the douche, similar to what are used in private families, may also be introduced over the bath tub, but there is little necessity for the formidable fixtures often provided. Unless a patient can be persuaded to take the shower bath or the douche voluntarily, its use is very problematical. Provision should be made for hip, foot and hand baths, and a few roller towels properly secured, with some flesh brushes, should be a part of the furniture of each bath room.

The floors of bath rooms that are much used, should be of smooth German flag stone or other material, that will not absorb moisture, and no wood should be used for wash boards. A strip of carpet laid in front of the tub when in use, will obviate the objection to the coldness of the floor, especially as all bath rooms should be kept well warmed.

WATER CLOSETS.—No part of the arrangements of our hospitals, even a few years since, were more imperfect than their water closets. A constant source of complaint, and a perfect nuisance in every part of the building where they were found, they gave so much annoyance that some practical men gravely proposed dispensing with them altogether. Our present knowledge of the subject, however, is such that they may be placed wherever they are required, and without their presence being known in the adjoining part of the ward. To effect this, it is necessary to occupy for the purpose a small room having an external window opening directly into it, to have the floor and other parts made so as not to absorb moisture, to use only iron in the construction of the apparatus, to have no basins or complicated fixtures to get out of order, and above all, to secure a steady and strong downward ventilation. All this can be done, and no reasonable expense should be spared to effect it. A special flue for each range of water closets, and an abundance of heat to secure an uninterrupted downward current of air through the receiver and discharge pipe, will well repay all they may cost; for with this effect produced, unpleasant odors in the wards from this cause are scarcely possible.

Where the water closets are near a flue of sufficient size, that is always heated, that may answer, and in private houses rarely fails to be successful; but if the slightest doubt is entertained, it is much better to provide a flue for that special purpose.

Various modes of letting on the water, have been suggested, and which answer the purpose, but I am disposed at present, to prefer that which gives a full supply to wash out the whole surface of the receiver, every time the door is opened.

Near the water closet, should be a *sink*, for washing various articles that it is not desirable to take into the bath room, and for obtaining water for the necessary cleansing of the ward.

The *urinals* should also be made of cast iron, well enameled, with a downward current of air through them, and have a steady stream of water passing over their whole surface, without both of which they are more likely to be a source of offensive odors than the water closets themselves.

A number of designs have been tried for permanent close-stools in the rooms of the most excited and careless patients, but none of them seem admissible which communicate with a common discharge pipe, unless a most thorough downward ventilation is secured through it. An enameled cast iron receiver, of suitable shape, with an opening at the bottom so small as not to admit a hand, firmly secured to a strong lid, and this locking as it falls on the top of a box, in which is a tin pan always containing half a gallon of water, will be found convenient and but little offensive. The whole box should be well fastened to the floor in a way that will allow air to pass freely under it, and tend to secure perfect cleanliness.

It is especially important about bath rooms, water closets and sink rooms that nothing should be boxed up. Every thing should be left open and exposed to view, there should be no harbor for vermin of any kind, no confined spot for foul air, or the deposite of filth, and all wood and every other material that will absorb moisture should as far as possible be discarded from the floors and from every other part.

WARD DRYING ROOMS.—Another source of annoyance and unpleasant odors in our hospitals for the insane, is that rather peculiar one, exhaled from the wet cloths and brushes so constantly required to be used, and which must necessarily be kept in the wards. To remedy this prevalent difficulty, which must be familiar to all who spend much time in the wards, it is proposed to have a series of rooms—one connected with each ward, or serving for two contiguous wards—thoroughly heated by steam pipe and with a good current of air passing through them, in which every article of the kind should be placed immediately after being used and kept till dry. The same room may also be used for drying various

wet articles of bedding or clothing which it may not be deemed necessary to send to the wash house.

WATER PIPES.—The great amount of water pipes used in a hospital
for the insane, their liability after a few years service to become defective, and the injury and disfigurement which fine buildings often receive
from this cause, make it very desirable that those that belong in the
same neighborhood should, as far as possible, be gathered together and
pass from the cellar to the attic in an open space sufficiently large to give
free access to them on all sides, for inspection and repairs; and so that
in case of leaks, there will be no injury done to the ceilings or other
parts of the structure.

It will be found expedient in most situations to use iron pipe for nearly
every purpose connected with the water fixtures. Its durability will
generally be found a sufficient recommendation, but as some water acts
on these pipes in a remarkable manner, it will be well always to have
them made of good size and of rather more than the ordinary thickness,
especially when passing horizontally for any great distance. Block tin
makes an admirable pipe for water, but is more expensive. Lead pipe
and reservoirs lined with that metal, for either drinking water or cooking
purposes, should be entirely discarded. Serious injury is thus often
done when least suspected, and all risk from this source should be avoided.

DUST FLUES.—A large tin flue, through which the dust, sweepings
of the halls, &c., may pass, should reach from each ward, or from points
contiguous to two adjacent wards, directly to the basement or cellar,
from which their contents can be removed when most convenient.

SOILED CLOTHES HOPPERS.—At least one of these should be provided
for every two contiguous halls, and through which all the soiled clothes,
bedding, &c., should be conveyed to the basement, preparatory to their
being taken charge of by those whose duty it is to convey them to the
wash house.

KITCHENS AND DISTRIBUTION OF FOOD.—With the exception of a
small kitchen for the use of the superintendent's family, one main kitchen
in the centre building is all that is required for the purposes of an institution of the size and character of that under notice. This position is
certainly the most convenient for this important room, and there can be
little question but that the proposed arrangement will be found most economical in reference to supplies, fuel, the force employed to do the
cooking, and for facility of supervision. The kitchen is the only room
in the whole establishment in which there will be a large fire, and it
should be arched for additional security and to prevent the steam and
odors from it passing through the floor into the rooms above. A large
ventilating shaft should be built expressly for the kitchen, and a strong

and steady upward draft secured by carrying up in its centre a cast iron flue of good size, through which the gas from the fires is to pass.

Arranged as proposed, this location for the kitchen can scarcely prove objectionable in any climate; for the heat, steam and odors will be promptly carried off, without interfering in any way with the comfort of the inmates of any part of the building. The very common annoyance from basement kitchens, has generally resulted from no provision being made for their ventilation, or if any has been attempted, it has been of the most imperfect kind.

Besides a cooking range and a rotary roaster, the main kitchen should have in it a complete steam apparatus for cooking vegetables, making soups, &c., constructed entirely of iron and tin, and with so good a ventilation that no vapor will escape into the room. A steam table for keeping up the heat of the cooked food and of the dishes, is also desirable. The steam for the use of the kitchen may be derived from one of the boilers in the detached building hereafter to be referred to. The best floor for the kitchen is the smooth brown German flag stone. Cement should be used for the wash board, and wood should be avoided as much as possible.

A *dumb waiter* should be provided for each series of dining rooms that are immediately over each other, so that the food and other articles required in the wards may be passed directly from the basement story into the dining rooms, or to points immediately contiguous to them.

The food, after being prepared in the kitchen, and put while hot in tightly closed bright tin vessels or boxes, should be placed on a car of sufficient size to carry what is required for one side of the house, and which is brought to a point adjoining the kitchen. When filled, this car is to descend so as to rest upon a railroad which extends through one of the cold air reservoirs from under the kitchen to the extreme wings on either side, and passes in its course the bottom of each of the dumb waiters. By these means the food is delivered promptly and hot to every part of the house. The refuse from the different dining rooms is in like manner to be sent down in closed tin vessels. Each ward should have a bell and a speaking tube, extending to the kitchen or other suitable part of the basement, by means of which whatever articles are required, may be called for without the attendants having ever to leave the ward for any thing from the kitchen, into which they should not be admitted.

HEATING AND VENTILATION.—There seems to be no diversity of opinion among those who have the charge of American hospitals for the insane, in reference to the proper mode of warming and ventilating these institutions; the "Association of Medical Superintendents" having unanimously resolved that "all hospitals should be warmed by passing an abundance of pure fresh air from the external atmosphere, over pipes or plates containing steam under low pressure, or hot water, the temperature of which at the boiler does not exceed 212° F., and placed in the basement or cellar of the building to be heated," and that "the boilers for generating steam should be in a detached structure;" while they also agree with equal unanimity, that "a complete system of forced ventilation in connection with the heating, is indispensible to give purity to the air of a hospital for the insane, and that no expense that is required to effect this object thoroughly can be deemed either misplaced or injudicious."

In the plan recommended in the present essay, it is proposed to place the detached structure alluded to, at a distance of not less than one hundred feet in the rear of the centre building. The precise position, however, will vary according to the character of the ground, and other circumstances connected with the different uses to which it will be applied. It may be at the distance of five hundred feet without inconvenience or disadvantage if the pipe conveying the steam is under ground and surrounded by some non-conducting substance. The boilers, of which it will be necessary to have four, unless they are of very large size, are to be placed under a shed with a slate roof and good skylights, adjoining the cellar of the detached building, and, if possible, sunk so deep that the condensed steam may return to them by simple gravity. If this can not be effected, the boilers must be kept supplied with water by a force pump driven by the engine. These boilers may be either tubular, which have the advantage of being easily put in place, requiring little space and generating steam very rapidly, or plain cylinder boilers, which are much less costly, quite as safe, and not so likely to need repairs. It is of great importance to have an abundance of boiler room and to use the steam under low pressure. The vaults for coal should be immediately adjoining the boilers, and so arranged that the coal may be dropped into them directly from the carts, while the ashes can be raised by a crane and windlass.

The steam is to be conveyed from the boilers through an eight inch cast iron pipe, till it reaches the air chambers under the centre building, and from this point a smaller pipe diverges to each extremity of the hospital. The radiating tubes may be either large cast iron or small wrought iron pipe. The latter is to be prefered on account of the greater facility with which it can be taken down or put up, corners turned and repairs of all kinds made, while the cost of it is no greater.

The radiating pipes should be prepared in three distinct sets, one or all of which can be used at pleasure. In the cool mornings and evenings which occasionally occur even in the summer months, and during the mild weather of spring and autumn, one series of pipe will be sufficient. With the ordinary winter weather, two will be required, and when the temperature is very low, especially if accompanied by much wind, the whole three ranges must be put in operation. This arrangement will be found very economical, and do away with all the difficulties sometimes experienced in the proper distribution of heat from a steam apparatus. So easy is it to control steam as a heating agent in the mode proposed, that there is no reason why heat should not be purchased in large cities or long ranges of buildings, as light and water now are. Such a suggestion was made by the writer some years since, and an entirely responsible firm was subsequently prepared to contract for the warming of the whole block of buildings on Girard Square, and owned by the city of Philadelphia, from one central apparatus entirely under ground. With such an arrangement, the occupant of a dwelling could have just as much heat admitted as he desired, by simply turning the stop cock which controlled the admission of steam into the radiating pipes in his cellar. The neatness, comfort and efficiency of such a plan, if once properly tried, would soon lead to its being extensively adopted.

For supplying steam to the hospital, kitchen and drying rooms, for forcing ventilation, pumping water, driving washing machinery, and heating water for all purposes, the different boilers may be used alternately in summer, and the pipe conveying the steam for the purposes indicated, should be protected by appropriate wrapping, so that no heat can be given out in the air chambers, to the annoyance of those in the rooms above.

It is recommended that the space under the corridors of the wings, should be made the hot air chambers, and the rooms on either side used as cold air reservoirs. The external atmosphere should be admitted into these reservoirs through various hinged windows, and from them into the air chambers by small openings about one foot from the floor, and formed by leaving out the space occupied by each alternate brick. The amount of cold air to be admitted, will depend somewhat on the severity of the weather, the prevalence or absence of strong winds and their direction, as well as upon the general efficiency of the apparatus. On these accounts, controlling windows are necessary. A full supply of fresh air, however, is indispensable to the proper working of any apparatus, and this should not be left to the discretion of any subordinate. The hot air chambers may extend the whole length of a wing, or be divided into shorter sections.

In arranging the radiating pipes, it must not be forgotten that a large amount of ventilation is required in every hospital, and that all ventilation in winter is loss of heat. A building not ventilated may be thoroughly

4

heated by one half the fuel required for one that is, but nothing can be more destructive to health than a residence in the former.

A common cause of failure in the experiments for heating in the manner recommended, has resulted from an attempt to effect the desired object with too little radiating surface, and with less fuel than is absolutely indispensable. There can be only a certain amount of heat obtained from a ton of coal or a cord of wood, and the fuel being applied to the generation of steam, can not alter the principle.

It is to be remembered too, that fresh air heated by steam or hot water on the plan proposed, can never attain a very high temperature, and of course must be introduced in much larger quantities than if from a common hot air furnace, and as a consequence, the flues must be very large and pass as directly upwards as possible from the air chambers. All lateral or sloping flues should be avoided. The flues frequently put into public buildings are not one fourth as large as are desirable. They should be made perfectly smooth on the inside, and the amount of air passing through them should be controlled by appropriate registers.

Although the heat from a hot water apparatus is entirely unexceptionable, and for private dwellings or small establishments even preferable to steam, still for a large institution like that under notice, steam is on many accounts more desirable. With steam, less radiating surface is required, because the temperature of the inside of the pipes throughout is nearly uniform, and never below 212° F., smaller pipes may be used, the heat is distributed and controlled with much greater facility and rapidity, and besides steam is required for various other purposes about the institution. The steam, too, may be generated at almost whatever point may be considered most desirable, even at a distance of several hundred feet from the building, and yet be conveyed to it promptly and with little loss of heat. Such a location for the boilers allows a proper site to be selected for the wash-house, gas works, pumps, &c., which should always be together, so that they may be superintended by the same engineer. It also protects the institution from one of the most common and dangerous sources of fire, and at the same time saves the inmates from all danger from explosions, and from the annoyance of the dust, dirt and gas connected with the fuel and ashes, and which, if in the building, are pretty sure some time or other, to escape into the rooms above. If hot water is used, it will be much more difficult to keep large fires at a distance from the building, and large fires in a hospital are always dangerous. By using steam as proposed, the only fire really necessary in the whole establishment, is that in the kitchen.

It is best that all the flues for the admission of hot air and for ventilation should be carried up in the interior or corridor walls, which being eighteen inches thick, will allow each flue to be about nine by twelve inches. In most of the wards it is proposed to introduce the heated air near the floor, and to have the ventilators to open near the ceiling. In the wards for the most careless and uncleanly patients, it will be well to reverse this arrangement, admitting the warm air near the ceiling and having the openings for impure air near the floor. When the warm air is admitted near the floor, especially when the patients are likely to interfere with the openings, a contrivance should be put up which would allow the air to escape freely and yet prevent any thing being thrown into the air chambers below.

The ventilating flues should terminate in the attic, in gradually ascending trunks of a size equal to the aggregate of the flues entering them, and leading to the different main shafts which rise above the roof of the building. The upward current in these shafts is to be secured by means of coils of steam pipe placed in them, or from the iron pipe carrying off the gas from the kitchen or other fires that may be used. Steam jets, fires in the attic, or gas burners, have some objections in a hospital for the insane, and as steam will be required for so many other purposes, its use, as suggested, will be found most desirable.

In addition to the several openings in the corridors, which should be numerous enough to secure the free diffusion of the air, there should be at least one for heat and another for ventilation in every room in the building.

Whenever a steady driving power can be obtained, fans are of all means the most reliable and effective for forcing ventilation. There can be no question as to the forcible displacement of air from every corner of an apartment by this means, and the steam engine may often be brought into use for this most important purpose. Even fans driven by hand are often very useful in some of the wards.

The great amount of ventilation required in hospitals for the sick or insane, renders it important that there should be a considerable excess, rather than any deficiency of radiating surface. About one superficial foot of radiating surface, the temperature of which is 212° F., will be required for every hundred cubic feet of space to be heated, in the latitude of Philadelphia. In some of the colder sections of the United States, it will require one foot of radiating surface to every seventy-five or even fifty feet of space to be heated, while in the South the ratio will be proportionably diminished.

The radiating pipe should be placed directly under the openings to the flues, and near them, so that all air passing upwards must come in contact with them.

To secure to each story and to every class of patients its due proportion óf heat, it has been proposed to have a distinct arrangement for each story, and this can not fail to effect the desired object; or the point in the air chamber, at which the flue commences will also regulate the supply of air to the apartment to which it leads. Without attention to these points, it is quite possible for the upper story to be over heated, while the patients in the lower one may be suffering from cold.

Although it is entirely inadmissable to warm a hospital by direct radiation from steam pipes, still, rooms that are not regularly used or only for short periods, as, for example, work rooms or halls or apartments that are particularly exposed to the admission of cold air, may have some steam pipe distributed in them to keep up the proper temperature, while the fresh warm air that is also admitted from the flues is relied on for ventilation. Great care, however, must be taken that this mode of heating is not so much extended as to interfere with the general ventilation of the house. In crowded wards, or in any part particularly exposed to impurity of the air, it should be entirely avoided.

Where the heated air is admitted near the ceiling and the foul air flue opens near the floor, it is particularly important that the windows should be tight and kept closed, to secure a regular circulation. There should also be registers in the foul air flues, near the ceiling, for use in summer weather or when the rooms have become accidentally over-heated. This mode of admitting warm air has peculiar advantages for the class of patients for whom it is recommended, for it not only prevents their congregating around the hot air openings and using the flue as a spittoon, but effectually secures the wards from all the offensive odors with which it is frequently filled from articles thrown through the registers. At the same time it must be acknowledged, that for those who are not addicted to these habits, there is great comfort in being able to approach the warm air when coming in cold and chilly, and subsequently regulating their distance from it as may be most agreeable to their feelings.

There is really nothing so pleasant or probably so healthful in the way of heating, as the warm air derived from an open wood or coal fire, with which there is never any deficiency of ventilation. If with this, a reasonable amount of pure and slightly heated air is admitted into the halls of a private dwelling to moderate the general temperature, and to prevent currents of cold air when the room doors are opened, we have the most comfortable of all modes of heating. Open fires would not be less pleasant in the parlors of a hospital for the insane, but the risks attending them at times, even in the least excited wards, are so numerous as to render it prudent to dispense with them in every part of the building regularly occupied by patients.

LIGHTING.—Every hospital should be lighted with gas, and the necessary pipes should be put in during the progress of the building. If gas can not be conveniently obtained from a company's works, it may be made on the premises without difficulty, by persons who are necessarily employed for other purposes, and at a cost that will render it cheaper than any other kind of illumination. In addition to the economy of its use, the thorough lighting of a hospital for the insane has really a remedial effect, and gas is certainly the safest, neatest, and in all respects, most convenient mode of effecting it. The retorts for manufacturing the gas can be conveniently placed in the basement of the detached building hereafter to be more particularly referred to, and the room can be thoroughly ventilated through the main shaft in its immediate vicinity. The gas holder should be of sufficient size to contain several days consumption, although it may be best for the works to keep them from getting entirely cold, by making some gas every day.

WASHING, DRYING, IRONING AND BAKING.—All these operations should be carried on in a building entirely detached from the main structure, and at least one hundred feet from it. Under some peculiar circumstances, the baking may be done in the hospital building, but ordinarily it will be desirable that it should be in the position first suggested.

The detached building should be about forty feet by fifty feet, and two stories high. On one side of it should be a shed, covered with slate, and well lighted from the roof, under which the boilers for warming the building, &c., should be placed.

The steam engine and the work shop of the engineer, should be in the basement of the building, and behind these, the room in which the gas is to be manufactured, so that the engineer can readily superintend all these processes. The main chimney stack will be at the rear of the building, and must be carried up to a height that will secure a good current of air to all the fires for which it is to be used.

On the first floor of this building in front, may be placed the bake house, baker's store room, and a stairway leading to the chambers of the baker, engineer and firemen in the second story. In the rear of the first story would be the wash room, containing a large cylinder for washing, and a centrifugal wringer, both driven by the steam engine, besides some permanent wash tubs, and a drying closet heated by air passing over steam pipe and driven through it with sufficient velocity by means of a fan worked by the engine. In the second story over the wash room, with which it communicates by a stairway, is the ironing room, in which besides the iron heater and mangle, should be another drying closet, made thoroughly effective by the means already suggested.

FARM BUILDINGS.—The character of the out-buildings required, will depend very much upon the amount and kind of land owned by the institution, and the mode in which it is cultivated. Under any circumstances where farming is carried on, it will be necessary to have a barn of sufficient size to stable six or eight horses and twenty cows, and to contain the hay and grain raised on the premises; a carriage house to accommodate the vehicles used about the hospital and the farm wagons; and a piggery for about forty hogs. A carpenter or work shop, and an ice house, will also be required. All of these buildings should be inside the general inclosure, although seperated from the patients' pleasure grounds, and care should be taken that the barn and piggery are not so near the hospital as to be an annoyance to its inmates.

Cost.—The cost of a hospital like that discribed, will vary in different sections of country, according to the price of materials and labor, and the facilities for manufacturing the various fixtures that may be required for the different purposes of the institution. The estimates for completing such a building at Philadelphia, as made by competent architects is $155,000. To this sum, I would add for the heating and ventilating apparatus, for bath and wash rooms, water closets, sinks, water tanks and pipes, cooking apparatus, washing and drying fixtures, bake room, and steam engine and pumps, $25,000. The cost of furniture for every part of such a hospital when full of patients, would amount to about $15,000. The farm stock, wagons and tools, and the different vehicles required, would cost probably $3,000 additional, so that exclusive of the farm, which of late has generally been presented to the State, either as a gift from benevolent individuals, or by some town desirous of having the institution near it; the entire cost of building such a hospital for the insane, providing all its fixtures and furnishing it in every part, would be, in this section of country, not far from $200,000.

In making an estimate of the cost of a hospital for the insane, I have felt no disposition to underrate it. Believing, as before remarked, that every State is bound by the double claim of interest and duty, to provide such establishments for the benefit of its citizens; and that the best constructed, best arranged, and most liberally managed hospitals are always cheapest in the end, I have rather been anxious that the public generally should understand that such institutions, from their character and objects, must necessarily be costly as compared with cheap boarding houses or alms houses; and that the cost of simply supporting life and preventing absolute suffering in the latter, can never be made the standard for the rate of expense of a proper custodial and curative treatment in the former.

It must be remembered too, as already observed, that these State hospitals are for all classes, and it has been well said, that various comforts and arrangements which are necessary to prevent some portions of the

No. 1.

PLAN OF CELLAR.

No. 2.

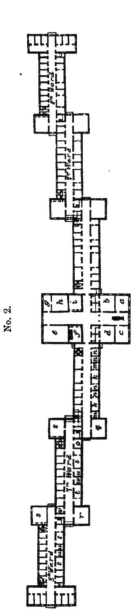

PLAN OF PRINCIPAL STORY.

community from feeling positive privations, are equally valuable as proving curative to their less fortunate fellow beings.

The difference in cost between a hospital that is well built, and one that is badly, between one complete in all its arrangements and one that is imperfect, between one liberally and one meanly managed, is really so small, that if the good citizens of any State would make the simple calculation how much of this extra expense would fall upon each one of them, it can scarcely be credited that a single individual could be found any where, who would be willing to admit that he would not cheerfully bear his proportion of it, even if it had never occurred to him that at some period or other, he might himself be compelled personally to test the character of the provision for the insane made by his State.

DESCRIPTION OF PLATES.—To render some of the arrangements which have been proposed more clearly understood, and to give a better idea of the style of building which has been recommended, the accompanying plans have been prepared. They were drawn for a State hospital intended to give ample accommodations for the officers of the institution, for all persons employed about the establishment, and for the custody and treatment of two hundred and fifty patients.

The building consists of a basement and two principal stories in every part, except the centre and the projecting portions of the wings, which will rise a few feet higher. On the centre building will be a dome, in which will be placed the water tanks made of boiler iron, and of sufficient size to contain 12,000 gallons.

The ventilating shafts will terminate on the projecting portions of the wings and in the central dome.

The centre building separates the two sexes, and on either side of it are three ranges of wings. The first range is separated from the centre building by a space, eight feet wide, with movable glazed sash, on each side of the passage, and the other ranges fall back just far enough to leave the corridors open at both extremities.

This arrangement, as will be seen, gives eight distinct wards for each sex, exclusive of some additional provision for very noisy or violent patients.

No. 1 represents the cellar excavated throughout its whole extent to the depth of seven and a half feet below the floor of the first story. The centre passage (a) is the hot air chamber, extending through the entire building, and in which the radiating steam pipes are placed. The spaces on both sides of this chamber are for cold air reservoirs, into which the external atmosphere is admitted through a portion of the windows marked on the outside of the building. In one of these air reservoirs is a railroad (r. r.) for conveying food from the kitchen to the different dumb waiters between it and the extreme wings.

No. 2 shows the basement or first story, which is raised two steps or sixteen inches above the ground. In the centre, is the principal entrance, with a broad flight of easy steps leading to the main story above. On one side of this entrance in front, is a reception room for patients (a), and back of it is the steward's chamber (b), on the opposite side is a parlor and dining room for the steward and matron (c), and back of this, the matron's chamber (d). These rooms are shut off from those in the rear by a glazed partition. In the rear, on one side, is the main kitchen (e), and a store room (f); on the other side, a small kitchen (g), a store room (h), and a dining room (i) for the female domestics and the hired men employed on the farm and in the garden. There are also two water closets in this story of the centre building.

In the first range of wings next the centre on one side, are two work rooms for the female patients (k), two store rooms for materials used and for articles manufactured in them (n,) two chambers for the superintendents of the work rooms (m), two ordinary store rooms (n), a bath room and a water closet, and the remaining small rooms are the chambers of the female domestics employed on the premises. The large room (q) is intended for one of the infirmaries for sick women, especially for those who are likely to be much visited by their friends or others, making easy access particularly desirable.

Precisely the same arrangement will be found on the side occupied by the males, so that throughout, a description of one suffices for both.

The second range of wings on this story constitutes the seventh ward for patients, and the third range the eighth ward. In both these, (r) is the parlor, (s) the dining room, (t) the associated dormitory or large room for a single patient and attendant, (u) is an attendant's chamber, and (o) a bath and wash room. The water closets, sink rooms, clothes rooms, drying rooms, dumb waiters, dust flues, soiled clothes hoppers, flues for ventilation of water closets, rooms for the water pipes, and all the other conveniences suggested in the foregoing pages, have been provided for in the larger plan, but its reduction to the size of a single page, has prevented their being distinct enough to have a separate reference. They are nearly all arranged for the accommodation of every ward, and those for two contiguous wards are grouped together as far as practicable.

At the extreme end of the eighth ward, and of those immediately above it, will be found on each side of the main corridor, three single rooms,—being six for the ward,—which open on a private passage way, and are intended for the most violent and noisy on the corresponding floor or for those whom, for any reason, it is desirable to have particularly secluded.

No. 3 represents the second or main story throughout. In the centre

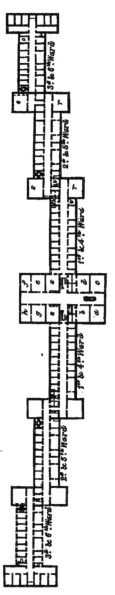

PLAN OF SECOND AND THIRD STORIES OF WINGS, AND SECOND STORY OF CENTRE BUILDING.

No. 4.

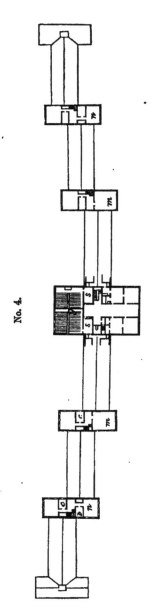

PLAN OF THIRD STORY CENTRE BUILDING, AND PROJECTIONS OF WINGS.

in front, on one side is a parlor (a), behind it, a room for visitors to female patients (b), on the other side, a managers' room (c), and behind it, a room for visitors to male patients (d). Both the rooms for visitors to patients, communicate directly with the adjoining wards. In the rear, on one side, is the general business office (e), back of which is the superintending physician's private office (f); on the opposite side, is the apothecary shop and general library (g), and adjoining it, the chamber of the assistant physician and apothecary (h). A small window forms a means of communication between the apothecary shop and general business office, and the wards of their respective sides, through the dining rooms (s), so that those employed among the patients may always communicate with the officers in the centre without leaving their wards. The fire proof safe is on this story.

Adjoining the centre building in this story is the 4th ward, beyond it, in the next range is the 5th, and in the extreme range, is the 6th ward. The general arrangements of all these are the same as have been already described for the 7th and 8th wards.

This plate also represents the story above in the wings throughout, being exactly like those below, and making the 1st, 2nd, and 3rd wards. The dining rooms (s) of the 1st and 4th wards, are in the adjoining parts of the centre building. The arrangements of the third story of the centre building will be shown in the next plate. The stairways for the wards next the centre, have been accidentally omitted in this plate, but they correspond with those shown in plate No. 2.

No. 4 shows the third story of the centre building, and the fourth story of the projecting portions of the wings. All the rooms in the front of the centre building, including bath room, water closet, &c., are appropriated to the family of the superintending physician, and are strictly private, one of the stairways from the second story being for their use exclusively. The other stairway for visitors and others passes up to the dome. In the rear of this story is the lecture room (g), which may also be used as a chapel, extending up through the fourth story, and having a direct communication with the wings of either side through the 1st ward dining rooms (s).

In the front of the first projection, is the museum and reading room, (m), and in the same part of the second projection is the school room (n). Both of these rooms have arched ceilings and sky-lights. Behind them, are the chambers of the night watch, and of the teacher (c.) The large rooms in the rear, on this floor, may be used for the sick, especially during the prevalence of a contagious disorder. The tanks containing hot water for the supply of the wards below are also in this story.

No. 5, (the frontispiece,) gives a perspective view of the entire structure. It will be observed that the usual portico, with high flights of steps has been dispensed with, as being costly, destroying the usefulness of the upper portion of the building, and not particularly appropriate for a structure of this character. The double verandah, which has been substituted, is to be made of iron, and being six feet wide, will make a good protection to persons getting in, or out of carriages, in wet weather, and form a not unsightly appendage to the building. The style of dome for the centre building, and the varied forms of termination of the several ventilating shafts, have been left as drawn by the architect, with the single remark, that if deemed expedient, something less costly may be substituted.

HEIGHT OF CEILINGS, WIDTH OF CORRIDORS AND SIZE OF ROOMS.— The height of the ceiling in the whole basement of the building, and in every part of the wings is 12 feet, in the second story of the centre 16 feet, in the third story of the centre, 14 feet, and in its fourth story, 10 feet. The ceiling of the lecture room is 24 feet high.

The main corridor of the centre building is 16 feet wide, the ward corridors, 12 feet, and the small passages at the extreme ends of the wings are 9 feet wide.

The main kitchen is 32 by 22 feet, the small kitchen 22 by 14, main store rooms 22 by 18, rooms in the centre building generally 22 by 18, the lecture room is 64 by 34, patients' parlors 20 by 24, patients' dining rooms 20 by 24, large rooms for patients with special attendants, 18 feet 9 in. by 11 feet, associated dormitories 18 feet 9 in. by 11, patients' single rooms 11 by 9, work rooms 18 feet 9 in. by 11, bath rooms 11 by 9, drying rooms 11 by 5 feet 6 in., fire proof passage ways between wards 11 by 5, water closet rooms 11 by 5, museums and reading rooms 34 by 24, school rooms 24 by 20, and infirmaries 24 by 20 feet.

The plan which has just been described, was prepared under my supervision and direction by Sloan & Stewart, Architects, of Philadelphia. These gentlemen are now superintending the erection of the new State Hospital for the Insane in Alabama, and have also furnished similar drawings for two new institutions in Ohio. To their taste and practical knowledge, I am indebted for valuable suggestions in reference to many of the arrangements of the building.

REMARKS ON THE PLAN.—The general features of the plan proposed in the present essay, were originally prepared by the writer at the request of the Commissioners for putting up a State Hospital for the Insane in New Jersey, and the designs for that building were made from the sketches at that time furnished its architect. Convenient, as most of the arrangements of that institution have been found to be, it is to be regretted that various modifications were made in the details of the original plan, which although diminishing its cost, impaired its completeness ; and the want of the last range of wings,—which are now in progress of erection—has always proved a serious interference with the comfort of its patients.

Many points of resemblance to the New Jersey plan, will also be found in the State institution of Indiana, at Indianapolis; of Illinois, at Jacksonville ; of Pennsylvania, at Harrisburg; and in those of Ohio, at Dayton and Cleveland; carried out, however, with very varying degrees of completeness. The State hospital now being built at Tuscaloosa, Alabama, is the only one yet commenced in which all the details and the whole extent of building recommended have been adopted at the very beginning of the work.

No proper estimate of the value of any plan for a hospital for the insane, can be formed, except it is judged of, as a whole. In reference to that under notice, I regard it, as every way important, that the building should be put up at once, of the full size recommended; and there is no reason to believe that such an institution will be found too large for any State, which has no other provision for its insane, with the single exception of Delaware.

If there was any doubt of the propriety of putting up the whole building at once, I should have no hesitation in saying that rather than leave off the extreme wings, it would be advisable that the work should be commenced at both extremities and made gradually to approach the centre; for the centre building could be dispensed with for a time with about as little inconvenience as those most important wards. It is quite probable, too, that appropriations to fill up such a vacancy between the wings might be more readily procured, than for adding new wings to the building.

The first patients sent to a State hospital, are very apt to be of the most noisy, violent or careless description,—those, indeed, who could no longer, without great inconvenience, be kept either at home or in the county jails or alms houses. For these patients, the extreme ranges of the wings are particularly desirable ; and without them, the classification must necessarily be very imperfect. Such patients occupying wards near the centre, render them to a greater or less extent, unfit for those who are expected ultimately to be received in them.

My own experience has satisfied me that the form of building shown in the plan, and carried out as suggested in the foregoing remarks, is every way preferable to any one which has wings passing off at right angles to each other. There is more certainty of the free circulation of light and air, better prospect are secured from all the patients' rooms and parlors, there is less opportunity for patients on opposite sides seeing or calling to each other, and less probability of the quiet patients being disturbed by those who are noisy.

As parlors are desirable in all the wards except those for the most excited classes of patients, and as the corridors are to have glazed and movable sash at both extremities, there does not appear to be any objection to rooms being on both sides of them. If there were to be no parlors in a hospital, and the corridors were to have their ends obstructed in any way, or were to be used throughout as sitting rooms, then patients' chambers would be admissible only on one side. Generally however, a ward having its corridor of good width, and not extended to an unreasonable length, open at both extremities and with rooms on each side, with their doors and windows opposite, will be found quite as pleasant, airy, and cheerful, and at least as easily ventilated, especially in summer, as one with a corridor closed at its ends, and rooms only on one side. A corridor thus arranged, with a double wall as it were on each side, can hardly fail to prove more comfortable in summer, even in a warm climate, than one which has its whole extent exposed to the direct rays of the sun; while the free currents of air passing through its entire length, and the transverse ones through each range of doors and windows, would seem to be all that could be desired. The plan of having rooms only on one side is necessarily a more expensive one, and throws the extreme portions at a greater distance from the centre of the hospital, for even if it is a rectangular structure, the distance is to be measured, as it would be passed over by a person going through the house, and not by an air-line from one point to another. The experiment of having rooms only on one side of the corridor, originally adopted in this country in 1817, has not been so satisfactory as to cause its repetition in more than two or three out of the 27 institutions which have since been provided for in the United States.

The proposed arrangements obviate the necessity of any mingling of the patients, unless perhaps to some extent in passing to the lecture room from the two extreme wings of the upper stories, when the patients must go through the wards nearer the centre, but as the patients from these will have already preceded them to the room, in which all will be mingled to some extent, no great disadvantage can result. In going out of doors, the patients never pass through any ward but their own. A classification that admits of no greater mingling of patients than this, is quite rigid enough for all practical purposes.

The arrangements for the most noisy class of patients is probably about as good as can be adopted. The extreme ends of the wings in each story being thus occupied, patients who become unexpectedly excited can be promptly removed, without having to pass up or down stairs, or under any circumstances, disturbing more than one quiet ward on their passage. Even in the most excited wards, it will generally be found that one or two individuals make nearly all the noise, and directly or indirectly cause most of the excitement among the patients. The six rooms, divided by the main corridor, at the extreme end of each story are so arranged that these patients can be comfortably provided for, and their noise or violence prove but little annoyance to any other part of the house. It is especially important to have means of classifying and subdividing, at least for short periods, the excited and the noisy, and also those who have an uncontrollable irritability and disposition to worry all who are near them. In no other position can these be better provided for than in that suggested in the plan, where they may be subject to a close inspection, as it is especially important they should be, and yet not seriously annoy the other inmates of the institution.

In conclusion, the plan will be found, it is believed, to give at as small a cost as can effect the object thoroughly, what was originally proposed as desirable in a Hospital for the Insane,—ample provision for the accommodation of the officers and all employed, every thing requisite for the custody, comfort and enlightened treatment of the patients, and arrangements throughout that will allow the supervision to be thorough and effective, and the management liberal and at the same time strictly economical.

ORGANIZATION AND GENERAL ARRANGEMENTS OF HOSPITALS FOR THE INSANE.

Important as it is in every point of view that the buildings intended for the custody and treatment of the insane should be constructed in the best manner, and furnished with every convenience calculated to promote the comfort of the patients and to facilitate their management,—still all these will result in comparatively small benefit to the afflicted, unless the system of internal organization and the general arrangements are based on correct principles and carried out with judicious liberality.

Upon most of the prominent points connected with this subject, there is believed to be nearly entire unanimity of sentiment, among those who have charge of the Hospitals for the Insane, in the United States, so that in expressing my own opinions on a large part of them, I have little more to do than to record the convictions which have been forced upon a majority of those who have had opportunities of testing practically the actual requirements of this class of institutions.

During a somewhat protracted connection with Hospitals of this kind, it has been my good fortune to be associated with Boards of Managers, and with assistant officers, whose views have so generally harmonized with my own, that our intercourse has always been of the most agreeable kind, and my suggestions have ever received that prompt and liberal consideration which leaves me no cause for complaints. For these reasons, as well as from a feeling that my period of service in the cause has been nearly as much protracted as can reasonably be required of one individual, and not knowing of any favors I am likely to have to ask for myself in the future, and being quite sure I have no past wrongs to redress, I shall deem myself at liberty to speak with entire freedom on this subject, without being chargeable with the slightest indelicacy, or of being influenced by personal considerations,—as much so, as though I neither had, nor expected to have any connection with such an institution. My only motive is to be useful to the insane, and the community, to save Boards of Trustees or Managers, the trouble and disappointment of resorting to experiments, which have been tried over and over again, and always with bad results, and to enable those who take charge of new Hospitals, to begin under circumstances that will allow them, from the start, to devote themselves to the welfare of their patients, and thus show the public how much good these institutions are capable of effecting.

Those who are hereafter to organize new institutions for the Insane, can scarcely be expected, in the commencement of their career, to be able to recommend what is most desirable, unless they have the means of comparing the candid sentiments and the results of the experience of those who have gone before them.

OFFICERS.—The officers of a Hospital for the Insane should consist of a Board of Trustees or Managers, as they may be called, and a Treasurer,—of a Physician in Chief, of one or two Assistant Physicians, according to the number and kind of patients under treatment, and of a Steward and Matron.

TRUSTEES.—The general controlling power over such a hospital, should be vested in the Board of Trustees, whose mode of appointment will necessarily be varied according to the character of the institution with which they are connected. In private charitable corporations they will be chosen according to the prescribed forms, by those duly qualified to vote,—while in State institutions, their appointment will generally be either by nomination made by the Governor, and confirmed by the Senate, or they will be selected directly by the Judges of the Supreme or other Superior State Court. The precise mode of election, however, is not of so much importance as the kind of men who are chosen, and that a determination should exist to prevent every thing like personal or political influences controlling their appointment.

The number composing this Board should never exceed twelve, while nine will often be preferable. Their tenure of office should be so arranged, that if changes are deemed desirable, the terms of only a limited number, should expire in any one year. Every one nominated for such a post, should possess the public confidence in a high degree, be distinguished for liberality, intelligence and active benevolence, be a man of business habits and able and willing faithfully to attend to the duties of the station.

The Trustees will have the general supervision of the institution and of its affairs, and they should at frequent stated intervals, either as a Board, or by Committees, make visits through every part of the Hospital, and exercise so thorough an oversight of its expenditures and of its operations generally, as will tend to secure the confidence of the whole community, and especially of those whose friends are committed to its charge.

One of the most important duties connected with the trust of these officers, will be the appointment of the Physician to the institution, and on his nomination, and not otherwise, suitable persons to act as Assistant Physicians, Steward and Matron.

The members of a Board of Trustees, performing their duties properly, are always able to exercise a most important influence on the prosperity of any institution, and in the welfare of its inmates; and they may also by injudicious measures, or a want of interest in its affairs, produce effects of an entirely different character. While giving the strictest attention to their own appropriate functions, they should most carefully avoid any interference with what is delegated to others, or meddling with the direction of details for which others are responsible. Especially should they avoid any personal interest in subordinates, that might lead them to a course that would weaken the authority of the principal of the institution. It would, indeed, be a safe principle to adopt, that there should be no ties of a personal or pecuniary character, between a member of the Board of Trustees, and those who are employed in any of the departments of an institution, which could at any time prevent an unbiassed judgment in a case of difficulty. Under no circumstances, should a Trustee so far forget the proprieties of his station, as to resort to subordinates for information that should come from the principal,—or to circulate unfavorable reports in regard to the institution, without having first informed this officer of their existence and tendency, and learned from him their truth or falsehood, as well as the reasons which may have induced acts, which although correct in themselves, might, without proper explanation, be readily so misunderstood as to do great injustice to innocent parties.

Boards of Trustees, while exercising the strictest honorable scrutiny of their officers, should be prepared, on every proper occasion, to give them a steadfast support in the performance of their arduous and responsible duties. They can thus add most essentially to their power of doing good. It is a great encouragement to those who are engaged in this vocation, to find their efforts properly appreciated by those, to whom they are directly responsible, and who ought to be most familiar with their modes of management and the beneficial results of their labors.

It is scarcely necessary to say that it is quite inadmissible for Trustees to have an interest, directly or indirectly, in any contract, with which the Hospital is concerned. Such a course may at least lead to suspicions, the existence of which, however groundless, is always to be deprecated, and might under some circumstances prevent a trustee from acting honorably and impartially.

Boards of Trustees should perform their duties without compensation, but the expenses actually incurred should be returned to them.

TREASURER.—The Treasurer should be a salaried officer, elected by the Trustees, and giving ample security for the faithful performance of his duties. He must reside in the vicinity of the hospital, but not in it; he should collect all monies due the institution, and should receive, hold and disburse all the funds that may come under the control of the Trustees.

He should pay the orders of the Steward, only when accompanied by bills of particulars, specifying the object of the payment, and certified by the Superintending Physician, as being correct, and approved of by him.

PHYSICIAN.—"The Physician should be the Superintendent and Chief executive officer of the establishment. Besides being a well educated physician, he should possess the mental, physical and social qualities to fit him for the post. He should serve during good behaviour, reside on, or very near the premises, and his compensation should be so liberal, as to enable him to devote his whole time and energies to the welfare of the hospital. He should nominate to the Board suitable persons to act as Assistant Physician, Steward and Matron. He should have entire control of the medical, moral, and dietetic treatment of the patients, the unrestricted power of appointment and discharge of all persons engaged in their care, and should exercise a general supervision and direction of every department of the Institution."

It will readily be seen how important is the task of selecting an indi-

vidual to fill the place, and to perform the duties, detailed in the foregoing paragraph which is in the exact words of the proposition, adopted
by "the Association of Medical Superintendents of American Institutions for the Insane." When once chosen, however, there would seem
to be no doubt but that his tenure of office and his compensation, should
both be such that a man of proper character would be willing to lay
aside all other engagements, to enable him to devote himself to the performance of his duties. Without good reason to expect the situation to
be permanent and the compensation liberal, no man possessing the requisite qualifications and talents, could be expected to give up his prospects of advancement in other branches of the profession, and so completely to cut himself off from the lucrative results of a successful general
practice.

Where it is possible to find a physician, who has already acquired a
practical knowledge of the details of hospital management and treatment, by personal observation and a residence in some good institution,
if joined with the other desirable qualifications, there is no question but
that such an individual is preferable to any other. If the Physician
chosen, however, has not had these advantages, he should be one that
is "apt to learn" and willing to embrace every possible opportunity to
make up his deficiencies, especially by a temporary residence in some
such institution, before venturing to take charge of his own. A few
weeks thus passed in Hospitals of the best kind, and devoted to a careful
study of their varied arrangements, and of their modes of managing the
insane, will save a Superintendent a great amount of subsequent labor
and anxiety, and result most advantageously to his first patients.

If the person chosen to occupy the post of Physician-in-Chief, is
practically familiar with Hospitals for the Insane, and has a taste for the
details of building arrangements, very great advantage will result from
his appointment being made before the commencement of the buildings,
and thus securing to the Institution the benefit of his experience in arranging the different parts of the structure.

It would seem to require but little argument to show that a Hospital
for the Insane should have but one official head,—in reality, as well as
in name,—to whom every one employed about it must be strictly subordinate. It would be as reasonable to suppose that a proper discipline,
or that good order would prevail in a ship with two captains, or in an
army with two generals-in-chief, or in a school with several principals,
as to expect to find them in a Hospital of the kind referred to, where
two or more individuals were acting independently of all others, or in
which there were certain officers over whom the Physician-in-Chief
had no control. If such an arrangement ever worked well anywhere,

it must have been owing to some very peculiar mental organization in those acting under it, and not because the principle was not radically wrong.

The very peculiar character of a majority of the patients received in such institutions, the numerous body of assistants required in their care, the large number of persons employed in the various departments, the necessity for active and unceasing vigilance, joined with gentleness and firmness in all our intercourse with the mentally afflicted, and for prompt decisions in cases of difficulty, render it indispensable,—if we wish the best results,— that a large amount of authority should be vested in the chief officer.

It must always be borne in mind that every department of a Hospital for the Insane, its farm, and garden, its pleasure grounds, and its means of amusement, no less than its varied internal arrangements, its furniture, its table service and the food, the mode in which its domestic concerns are carried on, every thing connected with it, indeed, are parts of one great whole, and in order to secure harmony, economy, and successful results, every one of them, must be under the same general control. It is not to be supposed that the Chief Physician of the Institution should personally superintend all or a majority of these matters, or fritter away his time in a constant attention to their details, or even that he should be proficient in every one of them; but it should be expected that he is so constituted, mentally and physically, as to be able and willing to make himself familiar with all of them, so far at least, as to know when every thing is in good order, and when all duties are properly performed. He should especially have that kind of tact and judgment, that will enable him to fulfill efficiently one of the most important functions of his office, that of selecting individuals for every department fully qualified to perform their appropriate duties.

It is a great error to suppose that there is any detail about the management of a Hospital for the Insane, beneath the dignity, or unworthy the attention of its Chief Medical Officer.   Every thing that has any relation to the patients,—and every thing has some direct or indirect connection with them,—may have an influence not readily appreciated by a careless observer, and to preserve unity of purpose nothing should be arranged or changed without consultation with the head of the establishment.

The Physician, who voluntarily confines his attention to the mere medical direction of the patients, must have a very imperfect appreciation of his true position, or of the important trust confided to him. He becomes in reality, a very secondary kind of officer, and his functions will be pretty sure to be considered by many around him, as quite subordinate in importance to those of some others concerned in the management of the establishment, which under such an arrangement can hardly attain, or keep a permanently high character.

No one will deny that the arrangement recommended,—which is the only one that can be relied on to work satisfactorily,—places much power in the hands of the Chief Physician, but it must be remembered too that on him the responsibility also mainly rests. A man to whom this amount of power cannot be safely intrusted, certainly is not the proper person to be placed at the head of an institution containing 250 insane patients.

The simple possession of adequate authority by the chief executive officer of such an institution, often prevents the necessity for its being exercised. It may be unseen and unfelt, and yet a knowledge of its existence, will often alone prevent wrangling and difficulties in the household, and secure regularity, good order and an efficient discipline about the whole establishment.

The long continued and uninterrupted performance of the duties of a Hospital Superintendent among his patients is a tax upon the mental energies, and ultimately upon the physical powers of an individual, not easily appreciated by those who have not had some experience of the kind; and one of the best modes of counteracting these effects, is for that officer to devote a portion of his time to the supervision of out door affairs. By this means, he will not only have the invaluable advantages of active muscular exercise in the open air, but also a kind of occupation for the mind, that will, more effectually than any other, divert it from the train of thought which had been induced by a protracted visit through the wards. Change of occupation,—both mental and physical,—is the relaxation of a Superintendent of a Hospital for the Insane, and is indispensable, if he expects for any long period to preserve his health and usefulness. So many noble spirits in our own country have already broken down, while engaged in the zealous performance of these duties, that hardly a better contribution could be made to the cause, or one that would more subserve the interests of the afflicted, than that which would aid in preserving the mental and physical health of the right kind of Hospital Physicians.

The nomination of the Assistant Physicians, Steward and Matron, by the Physician, will probably secure harmonious action between these officers, in the operations of the house. This point is one of great importance, and without it, there can be little satisfaction in the management of an institution. No Board of Trustees having at heart the prosperity of a Hospital for the Insane, could be willing to select or retain in office any of these named, who did not cordially aid in promoting the views and carrying out the plans of the chief executive officer.

In reference to all other persons employed about the patients, the power of appointment and discharge, as before observed, should be clearly and unconditionally with the Physician. A single interference with this power, could hardly fail to lead to acts of insubordination, and a disregard of the proper authority, and prove, to a greater or less extent, destructive of all good discipline.

ASSISTANT PHYSICIANS.—Assistant Physicians, besides being graduates of medicine, should be men of such character and general qualifications, as will render them respected by the patients and their friends, and able to represent creditably, or to perform efficiently, the more ordinary duties of the Physician, in his absence. As considerable responsibility will frequently rest on these officers, much more than simple medical attainments should be regarded in making a selection. It would be to the ultimate interest of the afflicted, and of the whole community, if the post could generally be conferred on those who are likely to devote themselves to this branch of the profession, and who seem to possess the kind of character, which in due time, would probably make them desirable Chief Officers of Hospitals for the Insane. They should especially be men of the highest moral character, of a cheerful disposition, but clear of frivolity of behaviour, and above all, they should be likely to be prudent in their intercourse with the patients. Although it must be acknowledged that some men make admirable Assistants, who are not so well calculated for Superintendents, still it does not often, if ever, occur that a poor assistant makes a good Chief Medical Officer.

Where there are 250 patients, especially if there is a large proportion of recent cases, two Assistant Physicians will be required, one of whom should perform the duties of Apothecary. In some institutions, one Assistant Physician and an Apothecary will be sufficient. If the full time of two Assistant Physicians, however, is taken up by their other duties among the patients, an apothecary may still be usefully employed in addition; and to him, other duties among the male patients may with propriety be assigned. It is, nevertheless, of great importance to the proper discipline of a Hospital for the Insane, that no supernumeraries should be allowed in any department.

STEWARD.—The duties of the Steward, and the importance of the office, vary materially in the different American institutions. In some, he not only performs the ordinary functions of that officer, but is also really the Treasurer of the institution, and receives and disburses large sums of money. The present essay, however, referring more particularly to State institutions, or those similarly constituted, the duties last named will be understood to be performed by the Treasurer, as an officer of the Board of Trustees, and whose duties have already been detailed.

The details of the duties of both Steward and Matron, with the sanction of the Board of Trustees, should be arranged by the Physician, to which officer they should be directly responsible.

The Steward, under the direction of the Physician, should make all purchases for the institution, keep the accounts, make engagements with, pay and discharge those employed about the establishment, and besides having a care of the farm, garden and grounds, should be able to perform many other important duties of supervision and police, that may with propriety be assigned him. He should give adequate security for the faithful performance of his trust; he should promptly pay into the hands of the Treasurer all moneys received by him on account of the institution, and should settle all demands,—except trifling incidental ones, for which he should regularly account,—by orders on the Treasurer, with bills of particulars, duly approved by the Physician.

MATRON.—The Matron, while having a general supervision of the domestics and of the domestic arrangements of the house, will also be able, under the direction of the Physician, to contribute essentially to the comfort of the patients, and all others about the establishment. Although the Matron will have considerable intercourse with the patients, her principal and most important duties, will be more connected with the housekeeping, while the general supervision of the patients, their instruction, amusement and immediate care will be directly and mainly confided to others, to be hereafter referred to.

Some able hospital physicians amongst us, have proposed having no Steward or Matron, but this suggestion, I presume, has arisen from the difficulties which in some sections of the country have so frequently occurred with these officers, and which have, no doubt, originated from improper persons having been selected for these stations, from their precise duties not having been accurately defined, or their subordination to the principal not being well understood, and it must also be added, occasionally from the very injudicious interference of Trustees, where difficulties have arisen between them and the Physician. Whether a Steward and a Matron are among the officers of such an institution or not, the duties commonly assigned them have to be performed by some individuals, whether acting under these or different titles. The terms used above are familiar to every body, and although those acting in these offices occasionally may not have correctly appreciated their true position, still I should scarcely deem it necessary, on that account, to reject these titles altogether. My own experience with Stewards and Matrons has been so fortunate, as to cause me to remember only their valuable services, and a pleasant official intercourse with them.

The individuals thus far named, are officers that can not be dispensed with, and are either appointed directly by the Board of Trustees, or on the nomination of the Physician. No reference, however, has been made to Chaplains or to Consulting Physicians, all of whom are occasionally deemed desirable. If either are appointed, it should be by the Board of Trustees on the nomination of the Physician.

CHAPLAIN.—In reference to the propriety of making the Chaplain a permanent officer, considerable diversity of opinion still exists among hospital physicians, the varied circumstances of different institutions leading their Superintendents to contrary conclusions on the subject.

The value of such an officer must depend almost entirely on the character of the individual selected, and the sound judgment and discretion with which he performs his duties. Under all circumstances, I have no doubt but that it will be found best that he should not be a resident of the institution. In addition to this, it may be sufficient to quote the language adopted by "the Association of Medical Superintendents of American Institutions for the Insane," viz : "If a Chaplain is deemed desirable as a permanent officer, he should be selected by the Superintendent, and, like all others engaged in the care of the patients, should be entirely under his direction."

CONSULTING PHYSICIANS.—It has occasionally been proposed that a Board of Consulting Physicians should be connected with Hospitals for the Insane, but this arrangement obviously could be of little service to the patients, and if it was intended that these officers should make regular visits, would on many accounts be quite objectionable. It is not possible for any one who sees insane patients only at long intervals, to prescribe properly for their ever-varying condition, or judge from short interviews, the real character of their cases; and medicines form so small a part of the remedies for the insane, that the wisest administration of them would be doing but little of what should be expected from a physician to such an institution.

Whenever from any cause it is deemed expedient to have Consulting Physicians permanently connected with a Hospital for the Insane, it should be with the distinct understanding, that their visits to the patients should be only in company with the Superintending Physician, and at his request, or at least, if desired by others, with his approbation.

With the selection or retention of any of the individuals hereafter to be referred to, the Board of Trustees can with propriety have nothing to do, all being employed in the immediate care of the patients, or in positions connected with the domestic departments, or the management of the farm, garden and grounds.

SUPERVISORS.—There should be one Supervisor of each sex, and each of these should exercise a general oversight of all the patients and their attendants on one side of the house, and thus form a medium of communication between them and the officers of the institution. These individuals being exempted from the ordinary work of the wards, and their duties being extended through all the apartments and grounds occupied or used by their own sex, will have great facilities for ascertaining the mode in which prescriptions and directions are carried out, and the patients' comforts and general condition are attended to. They should be persons who possess in a high degree, tact, intelligence, activity, and above all, true benevolence, with a feeling of sympathy and kindness for all the afflicted. They should be able to appreciate the views and wishes of the Physicians, and in all their intercourse with the insane, or those employed in their care, should act with such coolness and prudence under all circumstances, as to command their respect, and to impress upon them by word and deed, the great importance of a kind and enlightened course of treatment.

TEACHERS.—There should be for each sex, at least one individual of a kind, cheerful and affectionate disposition, with considerable mental cultivation, and of refined manners, who also without any ward duties, or more than an indirect supervision of the attendants, should be able, under the instructions of the Physician, to devote their whole time to the promotion of the comfort and happiness of the patients. This may be done by instructing them in some useful branch of learning or ornamental handicraft, by reading or conversation, by joining them in their walks, rides or work, by suggesting or assisting them in the different means of amusement and occupation, and by various other modes that will readily suggest themselves to an individual of the proper qualifications.

These individuals are intended to be companions to the patients, especially those who are convalescing; and they have been called Teachers not only because it is a convenient term, and that they devote a portion of their time to school instruction, but because it is hoped they will also teach the afflicted with whom they associate,—at least, to some extent,—the true character of the institution in which they are living, the value of their accommodations, the motives of those who have placed them there, and of those who surround them, and as far as they can, the road to health and happiness.

The proper performance of the regular duties of all the officers, and of every attendant, occupy so much time, that it is not possible in most hospitals as now organized, for any one of them to devote any considerable period of the day to a single patient, however desirable it may be to do so. An individual of the proper qualifications, who can at the right moment spend an hour or two with a timid patient, just arrived from home, to whom all are strangers, and who is distressed by the novelty of a new situation, may prevent days of sorrow, and perhaps thus aid most essentially, in the first steps towards a recovery. Judicious conversation at the right moment, a brisk walk in the open air, or simply directing a patient's attention to a new object, may tend most effectually to prevent a paroxysm of grief, or an outbreak of violence. The appearance of a new face, in whom all feel confidence, when the attendants in a ward are almost worn out by the long continued excitement of the patients, will often prove as great a relief to them, as to those of whom they have charge, and it is just at these periods that the presence of the Teachers will often be found most valuable.

One teacher of each sex has been mentioned as desirable in every hospital, but in those in which a large number of cases are under treatment, especially where many patients of cultivated minds are received, a larger number could be advantageously employed.

ATTENDANTS.—There should always be two attendants in each ward without regard to size, unless, as sometimes happens, two contiguous wards are so small and so arranged, that three persons can perform the duties of both. It should also be an unvarying rule, that, unless by special instructions from the Physician, one attendant should always be in the presence of the patients in every ward of a hospital for the insane. Where there is but a single attendant to a ward, the patients must have an insufficient amount of out-door exercise and employment, or those left in the house must often be alone, and the supervision must be altogether much less strict than is desirable. A certain amount of labor, out-door exercise and recreation, is as desirable for the attendants as for the patients. Work in the open air, with the male patients at least, should be a part of the duty of each attendant. Without it, those accustomed to active pursuits, are liable from the great change in their habits, to have their health impaired, their tempers rendered irritable, and ultimately incapacitated for the efficient performance of their duties.

The proper selection of attendants is one of the many important duties to be performed by the Physician, and it should be the earnest desire of every governing Board, to sanction all regulations that tend to secure to an institution a class of persons whose services are particularly desirable, and who seem from their natural character and their education, to be specially qualified for such a post. With all the supervision that can be given, the comfort of the patients in every Hospital for the Insane, is essentially dependent on their attendants.

The duties of attendants, when faithfully performed, are often harassing, and in many of the wards, among excited patients, are peculiarly so. On this account pains should always be taken to give them a reasonable amount of relaxation, and their position should, in every respect, be made as comfortable as possible.

The number of attendants proposed above, is deemed essential to keep up the proper supervision, and to carry out thoroughly the best system of treatment. The average is about one attendant to every eight patients, while the minimum that is regarded by the Association of Medical Superintendents, as at all admissible, is one to every ten patients. In some institutions, the proportion of attendants may advantageously be higher. Many hospitals commence with a less proportion of attendants than has been suggested, from a belief on the part of the Physician, that a larger number would be objected to by the Board of Trustees. I am disposed, however, to believe that this is commonly an error, and that if the matter were properly explained to any intelligent body of men, and its importance to the happiness and recovery of the patients, and the character of the institution, fairly insisted on, no intelligent Board would refuse their assent to the wishes of their chief medical officer. Under any circumstances, there can be no doubt as to the course proper to be pursued by this officer. He should ask for, and earnestly urge upon the Board of Trustees, whatever he deems right, and leave the responsibility and loss of having any thing less, with those to whose authority he is bound to yield, however much he may differ from them in opinion.

NIGHT WATCH.—An efficient night watch should always be maintained, wherever many insane patients are collected, and should consist, if possible, of a man and wife, to whom should be confided the charge of the male and female wards respectively. It is not simply to prevent accidents from fire, that a night watch is considered indispensable, although this alone is a sufficient reason for such a provision. When we recollect that the patients are in their rooms at least one third of the whole twenty-four hours, it seems surprising that while so much care is very properly shown in having them under constant supervision during one portion of the day, it should ever be thought justifiable to leave the same individuals, so totally unprotected and unguarded as it were, during so long a continuous period as eight hours. It is to be remembered, too, that during this period, the patients are commonly locked in their rooms, that they have no means of assisting themselves, no mode of securing prompt aid in case of unexpected sickness, except by noise, which disturbs others and does not always attract the proper attention, and that many of them are particularly subject to sudden and alarming attacks, for which assistance should be summoned at the earliest possible moment. The regular night watch, too, may render important services in guarding against suicidal attempts, in administering remedies that are ordered for patients who do not require a special nurse, in supplying drink or food, which will often effectually quiet a restless patient, for hours; in soothing by a kind word those who have become suddenly alarmed, or by simply making up his bed or allowing a patient to wash his face, to give sleep to one, who without these little attentions, might have been restless, and disturbing all around him during an entire night.

The night watch should also be employed to secure to the attendants, as far as can be, sound and undisturbed rest at night. Under any circumstances, the sleep of attendants will occasionally be disturbed by night services; but if they perform their duty faithfully during the day, the character of their occupation is such that without good rest generally at night, their tempers are apt to become irritable, and they lose that kind of interest in their business, without which they are of little value in the care of the insane. Besides all this, the night watch is often a valuable assistant in the police of the establishment, and is able to discover and report various irregularities among the sane part of the residents, which without such officers might never become known to the Superintendent.

It seems quite probable that great advantage would often result from having more than one individual of each sex on duty at night—night attendants, as well as those for day service. So large a proportion of the insane sleep indifferently, there are so many who would receive consolation from a kind word, or the occasional presence of a cheerful, sympathizing face during their long, dreary, wakeful hours, so many that ought really to have attention every night for their safety as well as comfort, that we may well inquire whether, with our best arrangements for the care of the insane, we have not often been somewhat neglectful of them by night.

The objection to a night watch, sometimes made, that they disturb the quiet of the wards by their noise, simply shows that incompetent persons have undertaken to perform the duty. Those who are passing about after all else have retired, should accustom themselves to open doors, and to do whatever else may be required, in the most quiet manner, always to converse in a low tone of voice, to discriminate between those whom conversation will quiet and those whom it will excite, and they should always wear woolen shoes when passing through the wards.

In addition to the individuals named, who are brought directly in contact with the patients, there will be required one seamstress for each sex, one farmer with two assistants, one gardener and an assistant, one carriage driver, one jobber, one carpenter, one engineer with two firemen, and a baker, besides the females employed in the domestic departments of the house.

A State Hospital will almost always have in its household many patients who can, advantageously to themselves, assist in the performance of much of the work in the wards and about the premises, and thus aid to a very limited extent in lessening the expenses of the institution.

REMARKS ON THE NUMBER EMPLOYED AND THEIR COMPENSATION. —The circumstances of different institutions and the classes of patients received, will, to some extent, influence the number of persons required in their different departments. So in regard to compensation, the salaries and rates of wages must be regulated, in a great measure, by the cost of living, the demand for the particular kind of labor required, the rates that are paid for other kinds of service in the vicinity, and of course must vary in different localities.

It is believed that all the persons who will be found named in the following list are required in the organization of a State Hospital for the Insane, with 250 patients, and that none of them can be dispensed with, without, to a greater or less extent, affecting the welfare and comfort of the inmates, and the best interests of the institution.

The salaries named are to be regarded as the lowest that ought in any part of this country, with which I am acquainted, to be offered for the kind of service that is required, rather than what should be given to the most competent individuals. More ought frequently to be given, and will often be required, to secure the proper kind of officers and assistants, especially attendants, and to induce them to remain for any considerable period in the service of the institution. In many large institutions, the compensation of the Chief Medical Officer should be at least from 30 to 50 per cent higher than what has has been named.

Many of the positions about a Hospital for the Insane, from the highest almost to the lowest, require persons of peculiar qualifications, and when such are found, it will be to the interest of their employers to secure their services, even if a considerable increase of compensation is necessary to effect the object. A thoroughly good and efficient officer or assistant of any kind may be more desirable to an institution, at a large salary, than a bad or negative kind of one, working gratuitously. While good officers and assistants are desirable in every department, not only on account of the direct performance of their duties, but also because their example never fails to exercise a favorable influence on others of a less decided character, so an idle, vicious, or faithless one may be worse than none, simply from all their associations producing unfavorable results.

It may be regarded as a well established fact, that although in a few institutions a liberal compensation is given, in many, the salaries are quite too low, and entirely inadequate to be depended on, to secure and retain the best kind of talent for the different positions. The services required about the insane, when faithfully performed, are peculiarly trying to the mental and physical powers of any individual, and ought to be liberally paid for. With the great demand for talent and labor that constantly exists in this country, it is not surprising that considerable difficulty is often experienced in finding the proper kind of persons to take charge of the insane, when less arduous and responsible duties are frequently so much better compensated.

When proper persons are engaged to act as the regular attendants of the patients, it will often be found desirable to secure their continuance for a certain period, by a yearly increase in their compensation; although it must also be acknowledged, that not unfrequently, even the best of this important class, after a long residence in a hospital, seem to lose their interest in their duties and to do better to engage for a year or two in other pursuits.

The services of certain of the officers, after a considerable residence in an institution, often become much enhanced in value, and it is to them a source of great encouragement to know that strict fidelity and industry are likely to be recognized by an occasional increase in their income. No Superintendent would hesitate to say that the services of his assistants after two or three years' experience, are often worth almost double what they were during the first months of their residence in the institution.

SCHEDULE OF A COMPLETE ORGANIZATION WITH RATE OF COMPENSATION.—The following list, as before remarked, is believed to include only those that are necessary about a State Hospital for the Insane, when containing 250 patients, and that is to be managed efficiently, viz:—

A Board of Trustees, ...Expenses to be paid.
A Treasurer, non-resident,.................Salary, $250 per annum.

53

One Physician-in-Chief,		$1,500	per annum,

with furnished apartments and board of family.

If living detached and finding his family,........$1,000 additional.

One First Assistant Physician,	Board and	$500	per annum.
One Second Assistant Physician,	"	$300	"
One Steward,	"	$500	"
One Matron,	"	$300	"
One Male Supervisor,	"	$250	"
One Female Supervisor,	"	$175	"
One Male Teacher,	"	$200	"
One Female Teacher,	"	$150	"
Sixteen Male Attendants,	"	$168	"
Sixteen Female Attendants,	"	$108	"
One Night Watchman,	"	$168	"
One Night Watchwoman,	"	$108	"
Two Seamstresses,	"	$96	"
One Farmer,	"	$200	"
Two Farm hands,	"	$144	"
One Gardener,	"	$200	"
One Assistant Gardener,	"	$144	"
One Engineer,	"	$240	"
Two Firemen,	"	$144	"
One Baker,	"	$150	"
One Carpenter,	"	$240	"
One Carriage Driver,	"	$168	"
One Jobber,	"	$144	"
One Cook,	"	$150	"
Two Assistant Cooks,	"	$100	"
Four Female Domestics,	"	$80	"
One Dairy Maid,	"	$100	"
Three Washerwomen,	"	$100	"
Three Ironers,	"	$100	"

Exclusive of the Board of Trustees and Treasurer, who are non-residents, this list will be found to embrace 35 males and 36 females, or a total of 71 persons, all of whom reside within, or in the immediate vicinity of the institution, devote their whole time to its service, and are engaged in the immediate care of the patients, in the domestic or mechanical departments, in the cultivation of the farm and garden, in the care of the grounds or in keeping the various buildings and fixtures in good order. The whole of this force can be fully and profitably employed, and if composed of the right kind of persons, under good discipline, and with a well arranged hospital ought to be able to give the patients a high degree of comfort and all the advantages to be expected from a liberal course of treatment. It is not to be denied that 250 patients, with a farm and large garden can be taken care of, with a less number of persons than has been recommended,—for unfortunately it is done every day,—but the more extended my own experience, and the fuller my reflections on the subject, the more thoroughly am I satisfied, that there is a loss to the afflicted and the whole community, by every such attempt to manage an institution with an inadequate force, much too great to be compensated by the paltry annual saving of a few hundred dollars, which may be effected by such an arrangement.

A very moderate degree of attention to this subject ought to satisfy any political economist or legislator, that if a cost of $3 per week is necessary to give every patient in a State Hospital for the Insane that kind of treatment which is most likely to secure his prompt recovery, a scheme of management which limits all his expenses to $2 per week must deprive him of many important advantages, and in its ultimate results must prove much more costly to a State, than what would have been effected by more liberal arrangements. It is well for all to remember that a low rate of weekly expense per patient is not necessarily in itself any proof of a wise and judicious economy, although it may occasionally be an attendant upon it. If the rate is so low, as to prevent the patients realizing the full benefits that are reasonably to be expected from such institutions, although it may be by some regarded as economy, it is unquestionably of a kind against which every true friend of this unfortunate class should enter a firm and earnest protest.

RESIDENCE OF THE PHYSICIAN.—The direct superintendence of every department of a Hospital for the Insane, being vested in the Physician, it becomes necessary that he should be exempt from ordinary private practice and should reside on the premises, either in the hospital, or in a detached building contiguous to it. His whole time being devoted to the institution, great additional labor must be imposed on him, if his residence is more than two or three hundred yards distant, and what is of still greater importance, he will not be able, without great inconvenience, to perform his duties efficiently or satisfactorily.

If the Physician's family reside in the Hospital buildings, their apartments should be made every way comfortable, they should be entirely private, and not exposed to visitors or those employed about the house, while a distinct kitchen should be provided for their use.

For various reasons, which I deem quite sound, but which it is not necessary to discuss in detail, in the present essay, it is very questionable whether it is always desirable that the Physician's family should be accommodated in the Hospital building, although it is indispensable that they should be in its immediate vicinity. This is a question often to be settled by the particular circumstances of an institution, and of the person who is to have charge of it. Where this officer has a family of children, it is clearly best, in my estimation, that the Physician should not reside in the institution. Fond as patients generally are of children, and safe as they commonly are in the wards, still it is not desirable that they should be permanent residents of a hospital, either for their own sakes or for the comfort, quiet and discipline of the institution.

It is not difficult to have a house specially provided for the Physician's family, not more than three hundred yards from the hospital, where they can be entirely private, see their own friends, and provide their own table, without interfering in any way with the institution, or causing any difficulty in the thorough performance of that officer's duties. With an efficient and trustworthy Assistant, Steward, Matron, Supervisors and Teachers, it has been my experience that no disadvantage results from this arrangement. The time of the Physician will, of course, be mostly spent in or about the hospital, and his own residence is so near that his presence can, at any time, be secured almost as quickly as if in a distant section of the institution. The Pennsylvania Hospital for the Insane, at Philadelphia, the Bloomingdale Asylum at New-York, the Retreat at Hartford, Conn., the Maryland Hospital at Baltimore, and the S. Carolina Asylum at Columbia, have this arrangement, and, so far as I know, it has thus far worked satisfactorily to all concerned.

It must be obvious, that the families of physicians may often be so circumstanced, that the most competent men might feel compelled, from private reasons, to resign their posts, at the very time when their services were most desirable, if they were forced to live in the hospital buildings, and this arrangement might also frequently prevent admirably qualified persons from engaging in this branch of the profession.

As already remarked, the greater part of the Physician's time will be, as it ought to be, spent in or about the hospital, but it is still important that he should have a spot out of it, to which he can occasionally retire— rare as the opportunity may be—for rest and quiet. An institution will profit nothing by having its chief officer so situated that he can have no moments of leisure, none for study and reflection, no hour in which he can occasionally get out of the sight of his charge, or no time to devote to his own family, whose natural claims on him ought not to be entirely absolved by any public duties. The character of his pursuits, if zealously and faithfully performed, makes some kind of change of scene and occupation more necessary than in almost any other vocation. Variety of thought and labor are rest to him, refreshing his mind, and enabling him to return to his post, with fresh energy and renewed strength. Trustees sometimes make the lamentable error of supposing that the more closely their Superintendent is confined to his post,—the more arduous his duties, and the less assistance he receives from others, the more benefit the institution obtains for what it pays him. Hospital Physicians are no more able to resist natural laws than other men; when long over-worked, their ability becomes lessened, and when compelled to spend their time in attending to unimportant details that could as readily be done by others, matters of vital interest to the sick and the institution must often be neglected, or be only superficially attended to. It will be found, I believe, that every well qualified Superintendent of a Hospital for the Insane is sufficiently disposed to devote his whole energies to the performance of his duties, and to give the institution the full benefit of all that he can in any way perform, with quite little enough reference to himself or those immediately dependent on him.

One very important effect that has resulted from the establishment of "The Association of Medical Superintendents of American Institutions for the Insane," and which has not been sufficiently referred to, is that these officers are thus compelled at least once a year to leave, if only for a single week, their regular routine of duty to visit new scenes, and meet new associates. No one, I presume, who has ever attended these meetings will hesitate to acknowledge that he has derived great benefit from this short relaxation, and that he has returned to his post with renovated powers and renewed zeal in the cause, to which his life is devoted. Without any special reference to the obvious good effects which must result from a frequent mingling of gentlemen engaged in the same pursuits, and the abundant opportunities thus afforded for profiting by the experience of the whole country, it may not be amiss to express the belief that is now becoming universal, that no Board of Trustees or Managers should ever allow their institution to be without a representative at these annual assemblages, except for reasons of the most urgent character. Much as their Superintendent may be personally benefitted, by being present, the institution over which he presides cannot fail to be doubly so, and no expenditure made by a hospital is more certain to be returned to it, in its increased facilities for the best treatment and comfort of its patients, than what is incurred for this object.

FURNITURE.—The furniture in the wards of a Hospital for the Insane, should be varied according to the class of patients, by whom it is to be used. Its general character, however, should be made to correspond as near as possible to what is used in private dwellings. Neatness, plainness and strength should be its prominent features; and for a considerable part of the buildings, what would be used in a plain boarding-house, would not be inappropriate. It would be well, however, in making a selection, to avoid projections and sharp corners as much as possible, and any arrangement that would offer facilities for self-injury should be omitted. Where patients are much excited, there should be little movable furniture, either in the rooms or in the halls, especially of a kind that could be used as weapons. A portion of the bedsteads should be prepared for being permanently secured so as to prevent their being moved, by which means many patients can use them who would otherwise be compelled to have their beds on the floor. It will also be desirable to have a few very low bedsteads for those who are liable to fall out of bed, and who can be protected by having a good soft mattress on the floor by the bedside. For very violent patients it is often the best arrangement to have the mattress and bedding on the floor, and to remove all other furniture from the room.

The parlors should be comfortably furnished, and the room of every well-conducted patient should have in it, at least, a neat bedstead, table and chair, and to these a strip of carpet and a small mirror may be appropriately added. Every patient who is not filthy or destructive in his habits should have a good bed, either a hair or husk mattress on a palliasse, as one of the means of inducing sleep.

Iron bedsteads, when made in the most approved manner, are in many cases preferable to those that are made of wood. If made of cast iron, they should be heavier than are commonly used, on account of the facility with which they may be broken. For violent patients wrought iron is much more desirable. It is a mistake to suppose that iron bedsteads are in themselves a security against vermin. Unless every hole and crevice is filled with white lead and putty, or something answering the same purpose, before they are used, they may become quite as troublesome as those that are made of wood.

Provision should be made in every ward for vessels to contain cool drinking water, easily accessible to the patients, so that no one shall suffer from thirst in warm weather.

The table furniture of the dining-rooms should be neat and strong, and white ware will commonly be found most desirable, which, with the ordinary round-ended case knife and fork, can be used by nearly all the patients. For a few, who habitually break whatever is sent to them, tin vessels may be substituted, and there is occasionally an individual to whom it will be safest to give a spoon instead of a knife and fork; but where there is a proper classification, where pains are taken to bring patients to the general table, and where there is plenty of good food and an efficient supervision, the number of this class will generally be very small.

CLASSIFICATION.—Although, in the description of the plan of building proposed for a State Hospital for the Insane, the different wards were numbered, still little has been said of the various classes intended to occupy them. The only point insisted on was, that there should be eight distinct classes for each sex. It will be found desirable, in practice, that the least excited—what is commonly called the best class of patients—should occupy the upper stories and be·nearest the centre building, while the noisy should be at a distance, and the feeble in the lower story; but it is impossible to give any general rule that will be satisfactory in all respects to a novice in the management of the insane. The best arrangement, after all, will be to associate in the same ward those who are least likely to injure and most likely to benefit each other, no matter what may be the character or form of their disease, or whether supposed to be curable or incurable. No one, of course, would think of placing the violent and the calm, the noisy and the quiet, nor the neat and the filthy, together; but there are many grades between most of these, and individuals of extremely different character, who, nevertheless, do well together. Variety is as pleasant to a hospital patient as to any one else, and even if it were practicable, it is not probable that it would be found satisfactory to have all our associates exactly like ourselves. Patients are often much interested in the delusions of their neighbors, and by their efforts to relieve the afflictions of others, frequently do much towards getting rid of their own.

Every one who has been long with the insane knows that some whose cases are chronic and considered incurable are among the most pleasant and agreeable patients to be found in an institution; they are most beloved by all about them, are noted for their refined courtesy and attention to strangers, and for their devotion to the afflicted, which make them regarded as treasures in the wards to which they belong. At the same time, of all in the house, many recent and supposed curable cases, are often for long periods among the most violent, careless or unpleasant patients, and in all respects the least desirable as associates.

SHOULD CURABLES AND INCURABLES BE SEPARATED?—The remarks just made, as well as those in a previous part of this essay, might perhaps be deemed sufficient to indicate my views in reference to the propriety or expediency of providing separate institutions for those who are supposed to be curable, and those who are regarded as not likely to be benefitted by treatment. As propositions of this kind, however, are frequently made, I desire to enter my special and earnest protest against any such arrangement. The first grand objection to such a separation is, that no one can say with entire certainty who is incurable ; and to condemn any one to an institution for this particular class is like dooming him to utter hopelessness. In any other disease than insanity, it would hardly be contended that its incurability was any reason for a neglect of treatment, where there was the slightest reason to expect even temporary benefit from its employment. While chronic cases are so often agreeable ones and recent cases so frequently not a little repulsive, it can hardly be said with propriety that the influence of the former on the latter is so generally injurious as to require their being placed in a separate building; to do so would often be cruelty of the rankest kind. A proper classification will remove every difficulty in providing for these classes in the same hospital. It is somewhat presumptuous for us to say that a recovery is impossible in any case. When patients cannot be cured, they should still be considered under treatment, as long as life lasts ; if not with the hope of restoring them to health, to do what is next in importance, to promote their comfort and happiness, and to keep them from sinking still lower in the scale of humanity. Fortunately, almost precisely the same class of means are generally required for the best management and treatment of the curable and incurable, and almost as much skill may be shown in caring judiciously for the latter as for the former. When the incurable are in the same institution as the curable, there is little danger of their being neglected ; but when once consigned to receptacles specially provided for them, all experience leads us to believe that but little time will elapse before they will be found gradually sinking, mentally and physically, their care entrusted to persons actuated only by selfish motives—the grand object being to ascertain at how little cost per week soul and body can be kept together—and, sooner or later, cruelty, neglect and suffering are pretty sure to be the results of every such experiment. When speaking of County Hospitals, I have already expressed my belief that the chronic insane can nowhere be properly taken care of at a less cost than in State Hospitals, which should be sufficiently numerous to accommodate all classes of persons laboring under this form of disease.

SEPARATION OF THE SEXES.—In every hospital the arrangements should be such that there should be little intercourse between the male and female patients, or the male and female attendants employed in their care. There will no particular disadvantage result from their attending religious services or lectures in the same room, but on other occasions it will be best that they should be kept entirely separate. The advantages of frequent social parties, in which the two sexes meet on familiar terms, are very problematical, and balls and dancing parties for the males and females together have appeared to me to be decidedly objectionable.— Most of our hospitals receive patients from all classes of society, and where there is this indiscriminate mingling of both sexes and all conditions in life, undesirable intimacies and acquaintances, in certain mental conditions, will often be formed that may at least prove somewhat mortifying to a sensitive mind after a complete recovery. Patients, especially females, should always be protected from everything of this kind during their residence in a hospital. For these and other reasons, lectures and entertainments of various kinds in the lecture room, where there is no communication between the sexes, or parties for one sex alone, will be found much more desirable than the assemblages previously referred to. If all the patients in a hospital occupy about the same social position, the frequent meeting of the two sexes might be less objectionable, but even then I should not consider it very desirable.

Where only one hospital is built in a State, it will, of course, be prepared, as shown in the plan, for patients of both sexes; and even where there are two hospitals, in entirely different sections of a State, it will still be desirable that both males and females should be accommodated in the same building, because the conveyance of patients from great distances to an institution involves much labor and expense, is often injurious to the sick, and is really in itself an evil of much magnitude which ought not to be unnecessarily increased. Where a community, however, is sufficiently populous to require two hospitals of the same general character in one vicinity, it appears to me there can be little question but that many decided advantages, and no disadvantages, will result from having one of the institutions appropriated to males and the other to females exclusively. Such an arrangement will secure to both sexes a more extended classification and much greater freedom, besides facilitating in many respects the general management of the institution. I have yet to learn of a single advantage that insane patients receive from having the two sexes in the same building, but I do know of many inconveniences and disadvantages which result from this arrangement.

RESTRAINT AND SECLUSION.—The use of mechanical means of restraint, and the protracted seclusion of patients in their rooms—although the former of them may be, and, as I believe, is occasionally desirable, but not absolutely necessary, in the management of our Hospitals for the Insane—ought both always to be regarded as evils of no trifling magnitude, and to abate which, as far as possible, no effort should be left untried. They both tend to produce a relaxation of vigilance, and it cannot be too often repeated, that whatever tends to make vigilance unnecessary is undesirable about a Hospital for the Insane. Besides leading patients into bad habits, the frequent use of the means referred to, in a ward, induces attendants and others to look upon them as a common resource in cases of difficulty or danger, to regard them as their grand reliance in every emergency, and to forget the great power of other measures that are entirely unobjectionable—the value of tact and kindness and sympathy in controlling the violence and dangerous propensities of the insane. And yet, without a proper force of attendants and an efficient classification, the use of mechanical means of restraint and the protracted seclusion of certain classes of patients is almost unavoidable.

Objectionable as I deem the use of restraining apparatus in a Hospital for the Insane, it can not be too earnestly insisted on, that it is no advance to give up mechanical means of restraint and to substitute the frequent and long-continued seclusion of the patients. Occasionally an individual may really be more comfortable and much better off in the open air, with some mild kind of restraining apparatus on his person, than he would be confined to his room without it; for this kind of long-continued seclusion is pretty sure, sooner or later, to lead to habits revolting in themselves and most unfortunate for the future prospects of the patient.

The subject is introduced here as a reason why no false notions of economy should be permitted to influence any Board of Trustees to ask the Superintendent of an institution to attempt its management with a force so inadequate as to compel him, against his better judgment, to resort to means so objectionable, and which are so destructive to the comfort and proper treatment of his patients.

LABOR, OUT-DOOR EXERCISE AND AMUSEMENTS.—Having referred to the unfavorable results of an habitual use of restraint and seclution in a Hospital for the Insane, it is proper to indicate in more detail some of the means by which these unfortunate effects may be obviated.

A properly constructed building, admitting of a liberal classification of the patients, and the employment of an adequate number of intelligent and kind assistants, has already been referred to as being indispensable for such an object. The design, in establishing every such institution, being the restoration and comfort of the afflicted, the relief of their families, and the protection of the community, there can be no question but that it is sound economy to provide everything that will effect these objects promptly and in the most thorough manner.

Without adequate provision for out-door exercise and occupation for the patients, and a liberal supply of means of amusement, the excitement of the wards, and the violent and mischievous propensities of their inmates, will be apt to be such as to require modes of management that might otherwise be easily dispensed with. The first cost of some of these arrangements will necessarily be considerable, but the ultimate results can hardly fail to be so gratifying as to satisfy the most rigid stickler for economy, that the only wise course is to provide liberally of everything likely to be beneficial to the patients.

The farm and garden offer admirable means of useful occupation to the insane at certain periods of the disease, for, useful as they are to a large number, no greater indiscretion could be committed than attempting to set all insane men at work in every stage of their malady. To those accustomed to such pursuits, as well as to many who have been differently occupied, regular moderate labor in the open fields or in the garden contributes most essentially to their comfort, and tends to promote their recovery. Labor, then, is one of our best remedies; it is as useful in improving the health of the insane, as in maintaining that of the sane. It is one of the best anodynes for the nervous, it composes the restless and excited, promotes a good appetite and a comfortable digestion, and gives sound and refreshing sleep to many who would without it pass wakeful nights.

The provision of adequate and comfortable workshops, in a convenient position, and under the care of competent superintendents, may be made a source of profit to an institution, and furnish another means of labor of an interesting kind to a large number of the insane.

The usual means of amusement, which demand active muscular exercise, should not be neglected. A Gymnasium, suitable in its fitting up, for insane men, and a Calisthenum for insane women, will be found useful. The various games of ball, the exercise of using a car on a circular railroad, the care of domestic animals, as well as regular walks on the grounds or in the neighborhood, are also among the kinds of exercise that will be enjoyed by many patients; while means of carriage riding seem almost indispensable for many, who from physical and other causes cannot resort to the more active forms which have already been referred to.

Within doors, the means of keeping a comfortable house are, in addition to the medical treatment. the constant presence among the patients of intelligent attendants, active supervisors and judicious teachers or companions, always ready to check the commencement of excitement, to separate quarrelsome individuals, and to change the train of thought of those who seem disposed to be troublesome. The means to effect the objects in view are very numerous, and the tact of an individual is shown in selecting those that are most applicable to a case.

The introduction of regular courses of lectures, interesting exhibitions of various kinds, and musical entertainments in the lecture-rooms of our Hospitals for the Insane, has done much to break up the monotony of hospital life, which is so common a source of complaint among the insane.

Regular courses of instruction in well furnished school-rooms, reading aloud by the teachers to the patients of the more excited wards, the use of well selected libraries, the inspection of collections of curiosities, the use of musical instruments, and various games, are all among the many means which an ingenious Superintendent will suggest for the benefit and amusement of his patients, and which ought to be provided for in every institution for the insane.

MEANS OF EXTINGUISHING FIRE.—In a previous part of this essay, much stress has been laid upon the importance, when putting up the building, of attending to every means likely to prevent the occurrence of a fire, or of its spreading, in case it should occur in any part of a Hospital for the Insane. These objects are to be effected by making the structure, in exposed parts, as nearly fireproof as circumstances will permit, and by having the building heated by steam, and all large fires kept at a distance from it. In spite, however, of all these precautions, a fire may occur from causes that could not be foreseen, and on that account, it becomes a grave duty for every body of men entrusted with the erection or management of such an institution, to see that adequate provision is made for all desirable means to promptly extinguish any fire that may be discovered on the premises; for no accident can be more terrible to contemplate than a fire raging at night in a building containing more than 200 insane patients, confined in their rooms, and utterly unable to escape without aid from others. Nearly all these accidents occur from the intense heat of large hot air furnaces, or from defective flues, or from wood being brought too near them; so that if, as proposed, steam is used for heating, and an effective night watch kept up, it would seem that every fire should be promptly detected, and that means could be readily provided by which it could be easily extinguished, almost without injury to any one. To do this, the large iron tanks placed in the attic of the building should always be filled towards

night; two large rain water cisterns should be provided near the building, and kept full of water at all times; there should be a fire engine
and six hundred feet of hose belonging to the institution, and the hose
should be so distributed that it could be attached to the proper water
pipes at the shortest notice on the occurrence of an alarm, and a large
stream of water be immediately directed on any point either on the inside or outside of the building. In addition, an iron pipe three inches
in diameter, should be laid at a proper depth around the whole building,
or at least on one side of it, and at a moderate distance from it; and, at
proper intervals along this line, fire plugs should be placed, to which the
hose can be attached whenever required. This outside water pipe being connected with that through which the water is forced into the
tanks in the dome of the building, all the water in them can be drawn
through the fire plugs and used, while the steam engine is being started,
and which, by closing a stop cock, can then be made to force the water
directly through the hose, upon whatever point is on fire. By proper
provision for a quick fire being kept on hand, the engine can always
be ready for working in less than thirty minutes from the time of an
alarm being given.

To secure prompt and efficient action in case of the occurrence of an
accident of this kind, it is important that those about every such establishment should be regularly drilled at stated periods to the proper use
of the different apparatus. The early discovery of a fire and its prompt
extinction is nowhere of more importance than in a hospital for the insane, for its inmates are more likely to suffer from the smoke than from
the heat, and on this account it is desirable that some provision should
be made by which the smoke may be to some extent prevented from
passing through the flues from the lower to the upper stories.

The mode of making the passage ways between the different wings
fireproof, from top to bottom, as proposed in another part of this paper,
will do much to prevent a general conflagration, and secure the safety
of at least a large proportion of all the inmates, under almost any circumstances.

SUPERVISION OF HOSPITALS FOR THE INSANE.—The best kind of public supervision for a hospital for the insane—that which will tend most
effectually to prevent abuses of any kind, to secure good management,
an economical administration of its affairs, and the humane and enlightened treatment of all its patients, will be found to be the regular visita-
tions, at short intervals, of a committee from a well constituted Board
of Trustees or Managers. Such individuals being men of benevolence,
high character and intelligence, serving without compensation, and
having no motive in giving their time and attention to the work, but a

desire to promote the best interests of the afflicted, forms the surest guarantee to the public, that no just complaint will pass without investigation, and no actual wrong go unredressed; while the frequent examination of the expenditures and the finances generally, will be the most effectual mode of securing a strictly wise and liberal economy in every department.

A permanently constituted Board of Trustees, or one not changed in a body, soon acquires a knowledge of the details of such an establishment, that cannot be possessed by a new set of men, and for this reason the visits from an intelligent board are much more likely to be thorough and useful than those made by persons who are comparatively strangers.

The only other kind of inspection of Hospitals for the Insane, that is likely to be at all valuable, would be that made by a commission composed in part, at least, of men practically familiar with the whole subject, and whose members should have characters so well established as to command the public confidence in their statements and recommendations. Where many private institutions exist, such a commission would seem to be especially desirable, and their visits could hardly prove unacceptable anywhere, if matters are properly managed.

The visits of large bodies, like grand juries, as commonly constituted, without any practical or professional knowledge of the subject, although it might gratify a certain kind of curiosity, could hardly be productive of any good result, either to the public or an institution, for their interests are entirely identical. The want of familiarity with the details of such establishments, of the peculiarities of mental disease or the best modes of treating it, would prevent such a body from making valuable suggestions; while the presence of so large a number of strangers in the wards at one time, might prove detrimental, and would certainly be objected to by many patients.

PROVISION FOR INSANE CRIMINALS.—Steadily increasing as this class unquestionably is, and important as every one must acknowledge it to be, that such provision as humanity and justice require should be made in every community, the subject is well worthy the attention of those about erecting State institutions for the insane, as well as of the Government.

Insane individuals are found in all our prisons, and, as might reasonably be expected, in a much greater ratio than in the innocent portion of the community. The relative number in the different prisons will be found really to vary much less than is generally supposed, except, from the circumstance that some States having no other provision for their dangerous insane, are in the habit of using their prisons as a place of safe keeping for most of this class. There is often an apparent difference in

9

the proportion in different prisons where none really exists, owing to the rigid scrutiny which is made in regard to the mental condition of every convict, in some; while, in others, if a man is quiet and able to work, no trouble is taken in regard to his mental soundness.

There is a certain class of old offenders and notorious prison-breakers, as well as dangerous homicides, who, whether sane or insane, should never be allowed to have a greater degree of liberty than can be found within the walls of a well constructed prison. Hard as this opinion may seem to bear on a few individuals, who have already taken or attempted to take life, or have deeply outraged the laws and the peace of society, still it is as nothing in comparison to the cruelty and injustice that would be done to a whole community, who had never committed an offence, by exposing them to the risks which must always attend the enlargement of such dangerous men, even during a lucid interval. There are many of this class who can never be safely at large, nor yet be kept securely in any hospital properly arranged for the treatment of the insane, without converting a part of it into a prison, or exposing the other patients to risks which no plea of that kind of morbid benevolence, which seems to regard with much greater sympathy the fate of a condemned felon than the sufferings of his innocent victims and their families, can ever justify. There are other cases, however, who occasionally get to prison wrongfully, persons who are not especially dangerous in their propensities, but who, while in a state of irresponsibility, have committed acts contrary to the laws, and who ought originally to have been sent to a hospital for treatment, instead of to a prison for punishment. Certain cases of insanity, too, that originate in prison may safely be transferred to a hospital for treatment, provided it is deemed expedient to remove convicts at all who become insane after entering a prison, and thus in a measure relieving them from the penalties of their sentence. If many of this class are received into any ordinary hospital for the insane, it can hardly be questioned but that the popular sentiment will be strongly aroused against the measure, especially as escapes will be of such frequent occurrence as to keep the neighborhood in a state of alarm, unless apartments entirely distinct from those of the other patients and of a different character are provided.

A writer of large experience in prisons and prison discipline has recently urged with great force, that it is very questionable whether, under any circumstances, an individual who has been justly sent to prison for the commission of crime should be removed from it till the complete expiration of his sentence. The certainty of every punishment fairly decreed by a court, is unquestionably one of the most important means of deterring bad men from the commission of crime. The deliberate sentence of a judge fairly implies that the offender is to take as a part of the penalty for his crimes,—with his deprivation of liberty and loss of character,—all the risk of suffering from ill health that may arise while he is in prison. The community, of course, is bound to see that no avoidable cause for the production of disease is allowed to exist in a prison, as well as to provide every proper means for its treatment when it occurs. All this can be done within the prison walls, whether the disease be insanity, or fever, or any of the ordinary maladies found in such institutions. Although to do all this properly may require a small hospital inside of the prison walls, still there is certainly no greater objection to that, than to converting a portion of a State hospital into a prison. One of the two alternatives must be adopted. It is very certain that many insane convicts may safely be allowed a greater degree of liberty in a prison yard than in a hospital for the insane, and it seems quite possible to fulfill every claim of justice and humanity by treating all insane criminals within a prison hospital. If it be deemed preferable, however, to send them to a State hospital, there can be no question as to the necessity of providing a distinct building for their accommodation. Even here classification would be important, but the individuals of this kind from a single State would not be a large enough number to justify a distinct hospital, as has been provided for this class in some parts of Great Britain. The experience of our State hospitals generally is decidedly averse to mingling insane convicts with the other patients, and the escapes have been very numerous in nearly every institution from which I have received any information.

VISITORS.—To secure the comfort of the patients and the good discipline of a hospital for the insane, it is highly important that judicious regulations in regard to visitors should be made and enforced. The propriety of the friends of patients visiting them while under treatment, will, of course, in a great measure, be left to the discretion of the physician. What is quite proper at one period of a case may be totally inadmissible at another. While at one time such interviews may be productive of much benefit, at others they may be decidedly injurious. When the first experimental visit has shown unpleasant results, it is hardly to be supposed that any real friends of a patient, after having had the matter properly explained, would wish again to incur the risk of injuring those in whose welfare they, more than any other persons, ought to be interested. There are but few individuals who should be allowed, even if willing, to incur this responsibility against the advice of the physician. Under ordinary circumstances, a parent could hardly be refused an interview with a child, a husband with a wife, a wife with a husband, a child with a parent, or a legal guardian with a ward. With those thus related, after the physician has performed his duty by a plain statement of the case, the whole responsibility of any injury that may be done to the patient should be made to rest. But with all others, unless very peculiarly related, the chief officer of an institution would hardly be justified, if, for their mere gratification, he permitted visits that he thought likely to prove detrimental. The interviews with friends should not be allowed in a ward, among the other patients, except in cases of severe illness.

In reference to the large class of visitors who resort to hospitals for the insane merely from an idle curiosity, the rules for their regulation should be made under the sanction of the Board of Trustees at the commencement of the institution.

In the vicinity of most public establishments of this nature, especially those provided by the States, there will always be found a large number of persons, who, with a kind of feeling of right, are anxious to have an opportunity of inspecting their arrangements. Carried to a reasonable extent, this kind of visiting is advantageous, as giving the community an opportunity of being disabused of old prejudices, and of knowing something of the science, liberality and benevolence which are now sought to be enlisted in the care of the insane. All this may be done, however, without keeping the wards in a constant state of excitement, or materially incommoding the patients, by the presence of strangers. Two or three hours in an afternoon, for example, during which only these visits might be allowed, would be sufficient for every purpose, and suitable attendants could, at these periods, be prepared promptly to wait upon company.

Large parties should rarely enter a ward together, for at such times there is seldom much satisfaction for visitors, and a crowd always tends to excite certain classes of patients. No visits in the wards should be protracted.

There are certain wards into which ordinary visitors should never be taken, because few of them would be able to appreciate the mental condition of their occupants, and the probability of serious injury to the sick would be too great to justify such an experiment for the mere gratification of this kind of curiosity.

No visitor should be allowed to enter a ward, or to pass through the private pleasure grounds of the patients, without the permission of the physician, and then should always be accompanied by an officer, or some suitable person selected for that duty.

The exceptions in regard to the parts of hospitals to be visited, as stated in a previous paragraph, apply to the Trustees or Managers, to official visitors of every kind, to the officers of similar institutions and persons specially interested in them, and the members of the medical profession. The first named have the right, and it is their duty to examine thoroughly every part, and it ought to be a pleasure to the physician to exhibit to all who have been named every part of his establishment, and to freely communicate the character of its arrangements and modes of treatment.

Official visitors, when thus making a minute examination of the condition of a hospital and of its inmates, may with entire propriety have a more free and unreserved intercourse with all the patients than can rightfully be accorded to any ordinary visitor. On this account, this kind of official visits should not be connected with those of other persons. The former have a right, although its exercise is not always expedient, to see every patient, whether they are willing or not; but it is a right that cannot be transferred to any other person.

It is not uncommon for visitors to make special requests to see certain patients, of whom they have heard, or with whom they may have had some acquaintance, and to exhibit disappointment, if they fail to be gratified. It is scarcely necessary to say, that no physician has the right, even if he had the inclination, to make this kind of an exhibition of his patients. Patients, indeed, who do not wish to be seen, should always have the opportunity offered them of retiring to their own rooms while visitors are passing through the wards. It would be about as reasonable for a stranger to call at a citizen's dwelling, and, from motives of curiosity, ask to see a sick member of the family, especially if delirious, as for an ordinary visitor to a hospital for the insane, from similar motives, to demand a sight of some individual, of whose name or history only he may have had some knowledge. Reasonable visitors, when told that the patients are not exhibited, that it is presumed they would not wish members of their own families unnecessarily exposed to the scrutiny of strangers, if unfortunately thus situated, and that such a proceeding is personally offensive to many, would at once see the force of the objection and courteously acquiesce in its correctness.

It would be well generally to impress on visitors through the wards, that those they see there are always to be treated as ladies or gentlemen would wish to be in any other situation, and that levity and rudeness of behavior is quite as objectionable, and childish and unfeeling remarks, or impertinent curiosity, can be as acutely felt and as accurately appreciated there as in a private dwelling.

The names and residences of patients should not be given to that class of inquisitive or thoughtless visitors who, after their return home, are apt to take especial pleasure in retailing the results of their observations on particular individuals, at places and in a manner, to render them particularly painful and offensive to the friends of those who have had the misfortune to come under their critical notice. When such curious inquiries are frequently and pertinaciously urged, it will be quite allowable to have a hospital name for each patient, for the special accommodation of this class of visitors. Such a course can hardly be objected to, when it is remembered, that even in well conducted penal institutions, no inmate's name is divulged to gratify an idle curiosity, and that a number is used in all ordinary reference to every individual.

ADMISSION OF PATIENTS.—While the legislature of a State is engaged in framing the laws under which the organization and government of its hospital is to be established, it is exceedingly desirable that there should be a specific, but simple provision made for the admission of insane persons into such institutions and for their retention and discharge.

The law should be so clear as not to admit of misconstruction, and should aim to have such provisions as will effectually secure to every individual his personal rights, and yet enable him freely and easily to avail himself of the advantages of such institutions, and at the same time completely protect those who have the insane in charge from vexatious prosecutions for the performance of their onerous and responsible duties. It is undoubtedly for the best interests of the entire community, and especially for the welfare of the afflicted, that all these ends should be equally and effectually attained.

Without wishing to enter elaborately into a discussion of this subject, which in many of its bearings is a most important one, and deserving of a more extended consideration that can be given to it in the present essay, it may be sufficient at present to remark, that a certificate of insanity from competent medical authority, after a careful personal examination, with a written request for the admission, from some near relative, friend or legal guardian, should be deemed indispensable preliminaries to the entrance of any private patient. The proceedings in regard to the patients sent by counties, or committed by the courts, will vary in their character, but should be such as will enable a benevolent citizen to compel those having charge of the insane poor promptly to transfer them from any place in which they are neglected, or suffering from the want of proper treatment.

It has occasionally been proposed, that no patient should be admitted without the sanction of a regular commission of lunacy; but such a suggestion shows a want of familiarity with the circumstances of a large majority of all the cases received, and the plan, if carried out, would be most oppressive and unfortunate in its results.

Those who have proposed this tedious and costly plan of proceeding can scarcely be aware that by it they would prevent a large number of most deserving and interesting cases from receiving the benefits of such an institution,—would cause others to be kept at home till the best period for treatment had passed, from the unwillingness of friends to give such publicity to their domestic sorrows and afflictions,—while on others, little able to bear it, it would bring an amount of expense, often greater than the whole cost of restoring a patient to health.

In the present day, many patients come willingly to a hospital for the insane,—some travel long distances alone and make their own arrangements for admission,—not a few, who are not originally willing to leave home, soon become sensible of the benefit they are receiving and stay voluntarily,—and many are restored in so short a time, that their absence from their places of business is hardly longer than is required for a tolerable journey, or would result from a severe attack of ordinary sickness, and may scarcely excite remark even from those who are in the habit of meeting them.

Of all the cases admitted into our hospitals for the insane, there is not really more than about one per cent., if so many, in which there could be the slightest advantage in having a commission of lunacy previous to their entrance; and these are cases with such a peculiar moral temperament, and so likely to give trouble in various ways, that all connected with them, as well as the officers of an institution, are interested in having them confined by legal process. But to subject the remaining 99 per cent., to the trouble, delay, annoyance and expense of a regular commission before they could be placed under proper treatment for their disease, certainly would not be adopting a rule of action that is to give the greatest good to the largest number.

The desire to have such preparatory legal proceedings has probably originated from a belief that the friends of the insane are disposed to confine them unnecessarily, or from sinister motives. A rather extended experience has satisfied me that this is not the case, the prevalent tendency being decidedly to postpone the period for this kind of action as long as possible, without sufficient regard to the best interests of the patient; and I have yet to learn of any deliberate attempt to confine a sane man in any of our hospitals, or to place an insane one there from bad motives. The possibility of all this being attempted is unquestionable, but that any such designs are often, if ever, entertained in the United States is very doubtful, and, if attempted, could hardly escape detection; for the officers of these institutions, regarding themselves as the special friends and protectors of the insane, would be the first to discover and expose such an outrage, and to brand those guilty of such a proceeding with deserved opprobrium. It occasionally happens that habitual drunkards, who are dangerous to their families, and are bringing ruin on all dependent on them,. but about whose insanity there is room for doubt, for the want of any other provision, are occasionally sent to hospitals for the insane, and these are the only class of individuals of doubtful insanity whom I have found any one desirous of confining in our hospitals; but although the motive is good, the propriety of their admission is quite questionable, for, as our laws now are, they can rarely be retained long enough to be permanently benefited, and generally their influence on other patients is not at all desirable, nor is their society deemed in any way complimentary by the insane.

The fact that the officers of our public institutions for the insane can have no personal motive or pecuniary interest in retaining any patient for an improper period, is now well understood, and has very properly relieved them, with all sensible people, of every such imputation. Deriving little credit for skill or successful treatment, but from those they send away, and constantly importuned by convalescent patients for a discharge, they are much more likely 'to err by yielding too soon to the wishes of ill advised friends, than by retaining a patient for too long a period.

When commissions in regard to the insanity of an individual are really necessary for the protection of his property—and this should be most sacredly guarded during his sickness—it would be a benevolent act, which would entitle its author to high honor, to render this proceeding less expensive than it now is; for, as at present managed, it frequently requires no inconsiderable part of a poor person's estate to enable any one to collect a debt or make a legal settlement of any business in which the individual may have been interested.

IMPORTANCE OF A CORRECT NOMENCLATURE.—The erroneous views of insanity formerly entertained, and the unfortunate modes of treatment which resulted from them, led to the adoption of terms which are now without meaning, and the continued use of which has an unfavorable influence on the best interests of the insane.

It seems especially desirable that this malady, now so much better appreciated by the whole civilized community than formerly, and the importance of the proper treatment of which is so generally admitted, should have every advantage that can result from a correct nomenclature. It is seldom that a disease so well recognized, so important and so prevalent, has had the misfortune to be called by so many ill-selected names, that have themselves tended to produce errors and confirm wrong impressions in the community.

Without any inclination to be hypercritical, it is proposed briefly to allude to some of these misnomers, which custom alone seems to have retained amongst us.

It must seem singular to any one who reflects on the subject, that the term "lunacy," as applied to this disease, should still be retained as generally as it is by the community, by the medical profession, and even by some of the latter whose labors in this specialty have done so much to promote the best interests of a large class of sufferers. "Lunacy" and "lunatic" are terms which have no meaning in reference to the diseases of the mind, and originated from a popular belief in influences that have long since been shown to have no existence.

Both these terms are particularly objectionable from their very derivation, tending to give wrong impressions of the disease and to perpetuate popular errors. Prevalent as the idea may have been with our ancestors, that the insane were specially under the influence of the moon, it is hardly to be supposed that such a sentiment is now seriously entertained by any considerable number in or out of the medical profession. If such are to be found, they would scarcely claim so decided an effect from lunar influence as to make it a ground for giving a name to one of the most important diseases to which man is subject. "Lunatic" is put down, in one of our best modern medical dictionaries, as "moon-struck," and such a term applied to a sick man or connected with an institution for the treatment of diseases of the brain, is certainly not in character with an age which puts forward so many just claims to be called one of progress. The fact that these terms are still used in law writings is no reason why they should be continued by the medical profession. If universally discarded by physicians, it is not unreasonable to suppose that the bar, with all its fondness for ancient terms, would ultimately reject names which, beyond their antiquity, have not a single claim for retention. As applied to individuals, they have become offensive from their ancient associations. The term "insanity," which I conceive is the only proper name to apply to the disease under notice, is a correct one; it simply means unsoundness, is sufficiently common, and its import generally understood.

With all its distinguishing features, insanity has nothing about it to prevent its being ranked with other diseases. A functional disorder of the brain, it belongs to the same category as those of other organs. Prevailing at all ages, among all classes of civilized men, without regard to talent, fortune or profession, there would seem to be no sound reason why the institutions specially provided for its treatment should have names different from those that are prepared for the relief of the sick suffering from other maladies. It is of great importance to a correct appreciation of insanity by the community, that it should be generally understood, that, treated properly from its commencement, it is commonly a curable disease, and that when patients are sent from home to an institution, it is only that they may have advantages and chances for a restoration nowhere else to be obtained. It should also be impressed upon all, that cases of insanity, however chronic they may be, or however discouraging their symptoms, should still be regarded as worthy of attention, and demanding treatment, if we can do no more, to promote their comfort and happiness, and to keep active, as far and as long as we can, their mental and physical powers.

Institutions for the treatment of other diseases, even if incurable, are called Hospitals; no other term is so common or so well understood, and there is none so appropriate in every respect to those devoted exclusively to the treatment and care of the insane, and, in my estimation, they should be known by no other name.

The titles often applied to institutions for the insane have no appropriateness, even if they do not have a mischievous tendency. The object of their original introduction would seem to have been to give an impression that those who entered them were not sick, or did not come for treatment, or, if ill, that they suffered from some malady which bore no relation to the other diseases which affect our race, but rather that they came as to a place of refuge or security, as though they had committed some crime, or been banished from the sympathies as well as the presence of society. It is quite true that, appropriate as the name of Hospital is for the institutions provided for the treatment of the insane at the present day, it could hardly have been proper to have so called the receptacles into which they were often thrown, much less than a century ago, where those who had the strongest claims for the sympathy and kindly attentions of their fellow men, were chained and flogged and treated with a cruelty far beyond the lot of most criminals.

The term "Asylum," still so common amongst us, seems to me to be open to all the objections that have been referred to, and ought to be abolished as having an undesirable influence, while its derivation and true meaning certainly do not offer any reason for its retention by any curative institution. It would be about as reasonable to have an Asylum for small pox, or fever, or dyspepsia, or any other disease, as for insanity. Ludicrous as it would appear to have an institution called a Febrile Asylum or a Rheumatic Asylum, it would really be as proper as to have what custom alone has familiarized us to—an Insane Asylum.

The arrangements of a Hospital for the Insane—which is a more euphonious, if not a more correct term than an Insanity Hospital—it is true, are different in many respects from those of ordinary hospitals; but that is no reason why the same name should not be applied to all.

The details of a hospital for children, for fever, for contagious diseases, or diseases of the skin, may also vary in their character, without requiring a change in their principal title.

The term "Retreat," is not less exceptionable than that of Asylum, and for the same reasons. They both originated from the best of motives, and have done good in their day, as helping to banish that awful name, "the Mad House," which, of old, had so many real horrors connected with it, and the truthful pictures of which in England and on the Continent have made such an enduring impression on the minds of men, that most of the popular prejudices existing in reference to modern Hospitals for the Insane, although they have no single feature of resemblance, will be found to have originated from this source.

The names of "cells" and "keepers," as applied to the chambers of the insane, and to their attendants, originated at a time when those who were suffering from insanity were often worse treated than convicted felons, and when those who had charge of them exhibited much less humanity than common jailers. Both terms belong to prisons, and no argument is needed to show that they ought never to be heard within the walls of buildings devoted to the relief of the afflicted.

If every one connected with the various establishments provided for the treatment of those suffering from mental disease, would on all occasions discard not only the terms "cells" and "keepers," and "lunacy" and "lunatic," but also those of "Asylums," "Retreats," and whatever other titles fancy may have suggested, and would call their institutions what they really are, Hospitals for the Insane, and let the disease treated in them be spoken of only as Insanity, the public would soon see the propriety of abandoning the terms to which exception has been taken, and that are in so many respects objectionable.

Few, if any, of those who have the immediate charge of the institutions for the insane in America, whose titles are deemed inappropriate, have had any agency in originating their names, and cannot, therefore, be held at all responsible for these unfortunate misnomers. Most of the new institutions commenced within the last few years in the United States are styled "Hospitals for the Insane," and it is well worthy of consideration by those interested, whether it would not be worth an effort to induce those who have the power to change the titles of those previously established, so as to secure accuracy and uniformity among American institutions.

APPENDIX.

At a meeting of "THE ASSOCIATION OF MEDICAL SUPERINTENDENTS OF AMERICAN INSTITUTIONS FOR THE INSANE," held at Philadelphia, in May, 1851, the following series of propositions relative to the construction of Hospitals for the Insane, was unanimously adopted as the sentiments of that body on the subjects referred to; and, in like manner, at the meeting held in Baltimore, in 1852, the succeeding series of propositions in reference to the organization of these institutions was also adopted, and, with the former, directed to be published in the "American Journal of Insanity," and to be appended to the annual reports of the different institutions:—

PROPOSITIONS RELATIVE TO THE CONSTRUCTION OF HOSPITALS FOR THE INSANE.

I. Every hospital for the insane should be in the country, not within less than two miles of a large town, and easily accessible at all seasons.

II. No hospital for the insane, however limited its capacity, should have less than fifty acres of land, devoted to gardens and pleasure-grounds for its patients. At least one hundred acres should be possessed by every State hospital, or other institution for two hundred patients, to which number these propositions apply, unless otherwise mentioned.

III. Means should be provided to raise ten thousand gallons of water, daily, to reservoirs that will supply the highest parts of the building.

IV. No hospital for the insane should be built without the plan having been first submitted to some physician or physicians who have had charge of a similar establishment, or are practically acquainted with all the details of their arrangements, and received his or their full approbation.

V. The highest number that can with propriety be treated in one building is two hundred and fifty, while two hundred is a preferable maximum.

VI. All such buildings should be constructed of stone or brick, have slate or metallic roofs, and, as far as possible, be made secure from accidents by fire.

VII. Every hospital, having provision for two hundred or more patients, should have in it at least eight distinct wards for each sex, making sixteen classes in the entire establishment.

VIII. Each ward should have in it a parlor, a corridor, single lodging-rooms for patients, an associated dormitory, communicating with a chamber for two attendants; a clothes-room, a bath-room, a water-closet, a dining-room, a dumb-waiter, and a speaking-tube leading to the kitchen or other central part of the building.

IX. No apartments should ever be provided for the confinement of patients, or as their lodging-rooms, that are not entirely above ground.

X. No class of rooms should ever be constructed without some kind of window in each, communicating directly with the external atmosphere.

XI. No chamber for the use of a single patient should ever be less than eight by ten feet, nor should the ceiling of any story occupied by patients be less than twelve feet in height.

XII. The floors of patients' apartments should always be of wood.

XIII. The stairways should always be of iron, stone, or other indestructible material, ample in size and number, and easy of ascent, to afford convenient egress in case of accident from fire.

XIV. A large hospital should consist of a main central building with wings.

XV. The main central building should contain the offices, receiving-rooms for company, and apartments, entirely private, for the superintending physician and his family, in case that officer resides in the hospital building.

XVI. The wings should be so arranged that, if rooms are placed on both sides of a corridor, the corridors should be furnished at both ends with movable glazed sashes, for the free admission of both light and air.

XVII. The lighting should be by gas, on account of its convenience, cleanliness, safety, and economy.

XVIII. The apartments for washing clothing, &c., should be detached from the hospital building.

XIX. The drainage should be under ground, and all the inlets to the sewers should be properly secured to prevent offensive emanations.

XX. All hospitals should be warmed by passing an abundance of pure, fresh air from the external atmosphere, over pipes or plates, containing steam under low pressure, or hot water, the temperature of which at the boiler does not exceed 212° F., and placed in the basement or cellar of the building to be heated.

XXI. A complete system of forced ventilation, in connection with the heating, is indispensable to give purity to the air of a hospital for the insane; and no expense that is required to effect this object thoroughly can be deemed either misplaced or injudicious.

XXII. The boilers for generating steam for warming the building should be in a detached structure, connected with which may be the engine for pumping water, driving the washing apparatus, and other machinery.

XXIII. All water-closets should, as far as possible, be made of indestructible materials, be simple in their arrangements, and have a strong downward ventilation connected with them.

XXIV. The floors of bath-rooms, water-closets, and basement stories, should, as far as possible, be made of materials that will not absorb moisture.

XXV. The wards for the most excited class should be constructed with rooms on but one side of a corridor, not less than ten feet wide, the external windows of which should be large, and have pleasant views from them.

XXVI. Wherever practicable, the pleasure-grounds of a hospital for the insane, should be surrounded by a substantial wall, so placed as not to be unpleasantly visible from the building.

PROPOSITIONS RELATIVE TO THE ORGANIZATION OF HOSPITALS FOR THE INSANE.

I. The general controlling power should be vested in a Board of Trustees or Managers; if of a State institution, selected in such manner as will be likely most effectually to protect it from all influences connected with political measures or political changes; if of a private corporation, by those properly authorized to vote.

II. The Board of Trustees should not exceed twelve in number, and be composed of individuals possessing the public confidence, distinguished for liberality, intelligence, and active benevolence, above all political influence, and able and willing faithfully to attend to the duties of their station. Their tenure of office should be so arranged that when changes are deemed desirable, the terms of not more than one-third of the whole number should expire in any one year.

III. The Board of Trustees should appoint the Physician, and, on his nomination, and not otherwise, the Assistant Physician, Steward and Matron. They should, as a board, or by committee, visit and examine every part of the institution at frequent stated intervals, not less than semi-monthly, and at such other times as they may deem expedient, and exercise so careful a supervision over the expenditures and general operations of the hospital, as to give to the community a proper degree of confidence in the correctness of its management.

IV. The Physician should be the Superintendent and chief executive officer of the establishment. Besides being a well educated physician, he should possess the mental, physical and social qualities to fit him for the post. He should serve during good behavior, reside on or very near the premises, and his compensation should be so liberal as to enable him to devote his whole time and energies to the welfare of the hospital. He should nominate to the board suitable persons to act as Assistant Physician, Steward and Matron. He should have entire control of the medical, moral, and dietetic treatment of the patients, the unrestricted power of appointment and discharge of all persons engaged in their care, and should exercise a general supervision and direction of every department of the Institution.

V. The Assistant Physician, or Assistant Physicians, where more than one are required, should be graduates of medicine, of such character and qualifications as to be able to represent and to perform the ordinary duties of the Physician during his absence.

VI. The Steward, under the direction of the Superintending Physician, and by his order, should make all purchases for the Institution, keep the accounts, make engagements with, pay and discharge those employed about the establishment; have a supervison of the farm, garden and grounds, and perform such other duties as may be assigned him.

VII. The Matron, under the direction of the Superintendent, should have a general supervision of the domestic arrangements of the house; and, under the same direction, do what she can to promote the comfort and restoration of the patients.

VIII. In institutions containing more than two hundred patients, a Second Assistant Physician and an Apothecary should be employed; to the latter of whom other duties, in the male wards, may be conveniently assigned.

IX. If a Chaplain is deemed desirable as a permanent officer, he should be selected by the Superintendent, and, like all others engaged in the care of the patients, should be entirely under his direction.

X. In every Hospital for the Insane, there should be one supervisor for each sex, exercising a general oversight of all the attendants and patients, and forming a medium of communication between them and the officers.

XI. In no institution should the number of persons in immediate attendance on the patients be in a lower ratio than one attendant for every ten patients; and a much larger proportion of attendants will commonly be desirable.

XII. The fullest authority should be given to the Superintendent to take every precaution that can guard against fire or accident within an institution, and to secure this an efficient night-watch should always be provided.

XIII. The situation and circumstances of different institutions may require a considerable number of persons to be employed in various other positions; but in every hospital, at least all those that have been referred to are deemed not only desirable, but absolutely necessary, to give all the advantages that may be hoped for from a liberal and enlightened treatment of the insane.

XIV. All persons employed in the care of the insane should be active, vigilant, cheerful, and in good health. They should be of a kind and benevolent disposition; be educated, and in all respects trustworthy; and their compensation should be sufficiently liberal to secure the services of individuals of this description.

Lightning Source UK Ltd.
Milton Keynes UK
UKOW06n1845200617
303754UK00001B/21/P